LIKE MUSIC TO MY EARS

A Hip-Hop Approach to
Social Emotional Learning (SEL)

Student Edition

By

Dwayne D. Williams

Printed in the United States of America

Cover design, text pages and layout: Dan Yeager, Nu-Image Design

Editor: Geoffrey Fuller

Like Music to My Ears:
ISBN 978-0-9847-157-4-9 (Teacher and student edition combined, paperback)
ISBN 978-0-9847-157-5-6 (Teacher and student edition combined, E-book)
ISBN 978-0-9847-157-6-3 (Student edition paperback)

Other books by Dwayne D. Williams
- An RTI Guide to Improving the Performance of African American Students
- Human Behavior from a Spiritual Perspective: Spiritual Development Begins in Your Mind. How to Achieve Success God's Way

Contact Dwayne D. Williams at:
Email: Dwayne@tier1education.com
Website: www.tier1education.com
Twitter: @dwaynedwilliams
Facebook: www.facebook.com/Tier1services

*This book is dedicated to all of my students who helped me understand
the effectiveness of using hip-hop to teach social emotional learning (SEL)
skills. Shout out to all students who were a part of my hip-hop movement
Tier 2 group and the hip-hop 101 after-school club.*

This one is for y'all.

One love,
Mr. Williams

CONTENTS

FOREWORD

DEVELOPING SOCIAL EMOTIONAL LEARNING BY PROCESSING AND ANNOTATING RAP LYRICS:

I have many amazing memories about the hip-hop SEL groups that Mr. Williams created. I am most grateful that, although he could have included any student to work with him, he decided to choose me to help him shape his programs and to share his vision.

The session I remember in particular was when we discussed the importance of social awareness, one of the 5 SEL skills. To address social awareness, we did not simply read from papers or books. Instead, Mr. Williams allowed us to listen to clean, edited versions of rap songs, and watch videos. For example, to shed light on the importance of social awareness, we listened to the song, "Black Zombie" by the rapper Nas. There are many different versions to this song, including a clean and edited version—the version without profanity—and an explicit version—the version that includes profanity. We listened to the clean, edited version, as Mr. Williams rarely allowed us to play explicit songs during group.

In the song, "Black Zombie," Nas challenges Black Americans to think for themselves and to deliver themselves from spells that have held them back for many years. In this particular session, group members annotated the rapper Nas's lyrics and talked about whether we were zombies—dead people walking and unable to think for ourselves. Members in this group consisted of all Black males. The lyrics that we annotated allowed us to discuss whether we blindly followed our peers, without considering consequences, and whether we know people and peers who were "zombies" as Nas described the term. In this session, we also discussed how unimportant it is for us to become attached to materialistic things, things that will not help us meet our goals in life.

Hip-hop SEL helped us absorb valuable information with our bodies—through engaging movement activities—and our minds—by processing lyrics, content, and ideas. Not only did we listen to Nas's lyrics, but also we critiqued his thinking and the thinking of other rappers.

During hip-hop SEL groups, we rarely had to sit in one spot for 50 minutes, listening to our teacher go on and on about information that was unrelated to our experiences; rather, we interacted and expressed our emotions. In our small circle, we created a family that confided in each other. We learned to trust each other, received advice from each other, grew with each other, and fed off each other. I feel like the group helped me realize that there is more than just me in the world to look out for and that I have the ability to lead in a positive mindset, regardless of what the news or any media have to say about the people who walk like me, talk like me, and look like me.

If Mr. Williams did not create hip-hop SEL groups, there would remain vaults locked inside me—I know this for a fact. He was able to make these groups purposeful and just as powerful as our mathematics, English, and history classes. What was different, though, was that he used hip-hop to drive the message home. He is bringing what is happening in our everyday lives to the classroom to help us identify problems and enhance skills that will improve our social emotional learning within the classroom and real world.

According to Pitchfork Media, hip-hop has contributed to about 35% of the best music made since 2010 and now students have someone in Mr. Williams standing up in their classrooms and school systems and saying, "Hey, this is what the kids are listening to today! Hip-hop is the vehicle we *must* use for those who already embrace it! Hip-hop is the vehicle we must use to increase engagement and to drive instruction—to get students from point A to point B."

—Marquell Oliver
Former Hip-Hop SEL Student
Hip-Hop SEL Facilitator

ACKNOWLEDGEMENTS

I thank God for giving me the inspiration and passion to write for countless hours about the need to consider nontraditional approaches to increase engagement among all students, including students of color. I thank my wife, Toni Williams, and children, Dwayne and Noni Williams, for their encouragement and support. I thank Dan Yeager and Geoff Fuller for their attention to this work. I also thank my former student, Marquell Oliver, for helping me create hip-hop SEL groups during his tenure as a high school student.

ABOUT THE AUTHOR

Dwayne D. Williams is a school psychologist, educational consultant, and certified success coach. He provides training to school districts on how to create entertaining instructional strategies to inspire students in the classroom. He also trains teachers, social workers, and school psychologists on how to create hip-hop groups for students, groups that focus on building self-esteem, confidence, and managing emotions. Dwayne earned a bachelor's degree in psychology (BA) from Fairmont State University; he earned a master's degree in psychology (MA) and an Educational Specialist degree (EdS) from Marshall University Graduate College. Dwayne is the founder of Tier 1 Educational Consulting—a firm that provides urban educational and psychological consulting services to administrators, teachers, community leaders, and parents. Dwayne is a first-generation college graduate. He was raised in housing projects in Springfield, Illinois, and often speaks on the need to connect with families and community leaders from underrepresented backgrounds. Dwayne is married to Toni Williams, and together they have two beautiful children: Dwayne II and Noni Williams.

Email Dwayne D. Williams at dwayne@tier1education.com
Website: www.tier1education.com
Follow Dwayne on twitter: @dwaynedwilliams

LIKE MUSIC TO MY EARS

A Hip-Hop Approach to
Social Emotional Learning (SEL)

Student Edition

NAME THAT SONG ACTIVITY

Name that Song for 1 Point
Name that Artist for 2 Points
Ready? Go!

This artist was a young talented rapper and producer. He was in a devastating car accident that resulted in reconstructive surgery on his jaw. The accident almost ended his career as a rapper. In fact, the car crash was so devastating that the rapper had to have his mouth wired shut. He was told that he may never be able to rap again. But the rapper was determined, so determined that, weeks after his surgery, and weeks after being told he may not be able to rap again, he made a song and "spit lyrics" while his mouth was wired shut! That's right, he spit through the wires that were placed in his mouth to hold his jaw together!

The following is one of his verses from his song about his car accident:

"If you could feel how my face felt, you would know how mace felt. . . .

Thank God I ain't too cool for the safe belt."

Name that song: _____ **(1 point)**

Name that artist: _____ **(2 points)**

CHAPTER 1: THE AMAZING OPPORTUNITY

Look, if you had one shot, one opportunity
to seize everything you ever wanted, one moment
would you capture it or just let it slip?
—Eminen, "One Shot"

Dear Student:

For the next few minutes, I want you to use all of your brain energy to think about a question that I am about to ask you. I really want you to think about this question, and so, if students around you are nagging you and asking you questions, please ask them to give you a few minutes of silence so that you could reflect on the important question that I am about to ask you.

If the neighboring peers do not provide you with silence, I will ask that you move to a different room. If you are in a classroom, ask your teacher if you could get about 10 minutes to read in the hallway or in a different location—away from the nagging peers.

If she doesn't let you, show her the sentence in this book where I ask that you find a quiet place to read what I am about to share with you; again, this should only take about 10 minutes. If you show your teacher the sentence from this book, she may agree to giving you time away to read this. Trust me, you do not want to miss out on this amazing opportunity!

All right, are you ready? Are you sure? Cool, here we go:

Imagine . . .

Imagine that the school psychologist in your building came to get you from class and explained that he wanted to meet with you in his office to discuss an amazing opportunity.

When you meet with him in his office, the school psychologist explained that he has been thinking about creating entertaining groups called *hip-hop social-emotional learning groups* and that he wants you to help him get the group started at your school. While talking with the school psychologist, he explains that he wants to create a group of 5-8 students and allow all students to meet in the same room, once a week, for about 30-45 minutes to use hip-hop music to teach social and emotional skills that will give you and other group members a better shot at meeting every goal you all will ever create.

As the psychologist explains the hip-hop group idea, he says, "You know, usually, when teachers create groups and opportunities for students to learn how to develop their emotions, teachers usually use boring books and do boring activities that students do not enjoy. And because students do not enjoy them, students tend to skip the group sessions, and when they do show up, they fall asleep, become disruptive, or use the entire group session to complain about how boring the group is."

As you listen and watch the psychologist, you notice that, the more he talks about creating this hip-hop group, the more excited he becomes. And so at some point, you interrupt his presentation and ask this question: "Okay—so you say hip-hop . . . well, how do you plan to use hip-hop to teach skills that lead to success?"

In response, the psychologist says, "Yes—I'm glad you've asked! Let me start out by explaining what I do not plan to do. I do not plan to use boring textbooks that are dry and have no connection to youth culture. I do not plan to have you all sit in circles and ask you all to explain your emotions to me and other group members. I do not plan to lecture at you all to the point I put you all to sleep. In fact, instead of

14

lecturing, I plan to use music to make our group sessions entertaining.

Not only do I plan to use music, but also, I plan to allow you and your group members to create your own music, write your own rap songs, and produce your own music videos! I plan to make this group the most fun and entertaining group or class you have ever been a part of!"

As you, the student, listen to the school psychologist go on and on about this "hip-hop group," you ask him to give you additional examples of the things you all will do in this group.

In response to your feedback, the psychologist leaps out of his chair and snatches two light gray pieces of paper with bullet points, jumps back into his chair, then slides you a copy. He then says, "Here is a list of bullet points that I have been working on. These are my thoughts on paper, and I want to get your feedback to add to my list to make the hip-hop group more interesting!"

With expression and excitement, he reads the bullet points aloud:

- We will use hip-hop activities and icebreakers to learn how to develop our emotions, gain confidence in our abilities, and enhance self-esteem!
- We will analyze hip-hop lyrics, and use examples from hip-hop culture to show how to increase motivation!
- We will develop our critical thinking skills by allowing group members to debate about "old-school" rap and "new-school" rap!
- We will create poetry and write lyrics about the information that we discuss in groups!
- If students want to engage in live performance, we will allow you all to perform the written expression within the group and perform for different classes throughout the school day!
- We will create fun after-school events in which our hip-hop group teaches the entire school staff about hip-hop culture, why we listen to hip-hop, and why hip-hop should be used in the classroom to make learning fun.

- We will allow group members to perform their rap music during school pep assemblies and within the community!
- We will change the game of education and start using hip-hop music to teach skills!

Now—Here Is Your Amazing Opportunity!

After reviewing this list with you, your psychologist looks you straight in your eyes. As he stares intently at you, without blinking, he asks you this question:

"Will you help me create this group?"

Are You Down?

What do you say to your psychologist? How do you respond to his question? Will you help him create the hip-hop group that he passionately discussed with you, a group where you and your friends could meet once a week to use hip-hop music to develop confidence, self-esteem, and critical thinking skills?

True Story

The amazing opportunity in the above scenario actually happened. Recall that, in the story, the school psychologist invited you to his office to discuss the possibility of creating a hip-hop group that would be extremely entertaining. Although I did not introduce myself in the story, I was actually the school psychologist and you—the reader—represent one of my students with whom I worked.

I had this amazing idea about combining hip-hop music with teaching students how to gain confidence and manage their emotions. I jotted my ideas on paper, identified hip-hop songs, documentaries, and videos that I could use within my groups and invited a student to my office to share my idea with him.

From the hip-hop idea, the student became extremely excited and asked to co-lead the group with me. I created this group at a high school just about 40 miles outside of Chicago, Illinois, and the group was a huge success!

We called the group, "A Hip-Hop Movement." The goal was to have about 5-8 students participate in this group, and when the group ended, create another group, and add 5-8 different students. We would do this for the entire school year.

Well, once students heard about *A Hip-Hop Movement*, many of them wanted to join. Because I had a long list of names of students who wanted to participate, I decided to create an after-school club where anyone could come out and enjoy themselves, by learning through hip-hop. We called the after-school club, "Hip-Hop 101."

Students met in this group—and in the after-school club, where they wrote music, debated about hip-hop, talked about their favorite rap artist, gained self-awareness skills, learned how to create and maintain meaningful relationships with their teachers and others, and discussed the importance of making responsible decisions.

My Purpose for Writing This Book

If you had one attempt at guessing why I wrote this book, what would you guess? Let's imagine that you have the chance to win $100,000 if you guess the correct answer. What is your guess?

Chi-ching!

Yep—one reason for writing this book is to share my ideas with you to see if you would be interested in creating a hip-hop group in your school, a group where you and your friends could use hip-hop to learn skills that lead to success, just as we did in the schools where I worked.

Keep it real, would you have won the $100,000 or was your guess way off?

I have a vision for changing the way students learn in the classroom.

Students have told me that their classes are boring and that, if instruction was more interesting and more relevant to their lives, they would be more motivated to apply themselves in the classroom and more inspired to do well academically.

A second reason for writing this book was to help you gain the skills that you need to be successful in every area of your life. That is, even if you do not collaborate with someone at your school or within your organization to create hip-hop groups, I will teach you skills that, if you read this entire book and apply the principles, could change your life forever!

To summarize, I wrote this book for two reasons: the first reason was to see if you would be interested in creating a hip-hop group in your school, and if so, this book will provide you with brilliant ideas on how to get a powerful group started, with the assistance of a staff in your school. If you are a part of a community organization, you could also start a group within your organization, with the help of a staff member. If you are interested in doing this, you could read this book and share the book idea—including the hip-hop group idea—with the teachers you believe will help you create the group.

If the teacher you choose to work with is too busy, you may want to talk with your building principal about how to get these groups started. If you are serious about getting these groups started, you will have to be persistent; this means that you cannot give up. If you run out of ideas and are serious about creating these groups, then email me. My email address is Dwayne@tier1education.com. I'll respond to your email with more ideas to consider, ideas that will help you connect with the right people in your building to get these groups started.

I have created two different versions of this book. I created this version for you and for students like you who may be interested in creating hip-hop groups to learn how to build confidence and how to manage emotions. I also created a version for teachers, school psychologists, social workers, and other staff members who are interested in learning about creating hip-hop groups to teach social emotional skills. The plan is to provide an adult with the adult version, and to provide the student with the student version, and have both, the adult and student, learn how to create these groups together.

My second reason for writing this book is to help you develop skills that may help you achieve every goal that you will ever create—and of course, I am speaking of goals that will help you be successful in life!

What Is in This Book?

Stories. In this book, I share a story about a student who I'll call Bobby. Bobby hated school so much that he would skip class and refuse to come to school. Bobby raked up a tremendous amount of referrals, detentions, and suspensions because he did not come to school. When I met with Bobby to learn why he skipped school, he shared a story with me that brought tears to my eyes. I share Bobby's story in this book, and I am sure that you can relate to him; if you can't relate to his story personally, I'm sure that you know someone who could.

I also share my story with you and explain how I overcame many obstacles that could have resulted in my dropping out of school, joining gangs, selling drugs, getting locked up, and perhaps, getting shot up in the streets. I share my experiences with living in housing projects, living in poverty, being held back in the first grade because I couldn't read, getting into fights in middle and high school, and hating school, just as Bobby hated school. I am sure that you know someone whose experiences resemble mine with hating school as well.

Social Emotional Learning Activities. I will discuss important skills that everyone should learn. In fact, psychologists now say that, if we learn these skills—not just students, but adults as well—then we have a greater chance at success in life. We call these skills social emotional learning skills, and I will focus on five of these skills to help you reach any and every goal you may have, whether your goal is about becoming better at reading, writing, math, sports, rapping, producing, dating, succeeding, sleeping, eating, bathing, walking—whatever! These skills will also help you become a better son, daughter, wife, husband, mother, father, businessman, businesswoman, teacher, coach, entrepreneur, lawyer, judge, police officer, professional sport player, engineer, and on and on. . . . I think you get the point.

In other words, if you learn these skills, you could do just about anything you are capable of doing. And when I say that these skills will give you a better shot at achieving any goal you will ever create, I am referring to goals that you are capable of achieving.

Okay, you need an example? Cool. For instance, if you have been cut from the basketball team each year during your high school career, then these skills may not help you get drafted into the NBA. There are many things you need to play professional basketball, things other than knowing how to manage your emotions. But if you have the basketball intelligence and skills to play in the league, then learning these skills and applying them will give you a better shot at getting you there! You know what I'm saying?

SEL skills will help you deal with failure better. Failure is a part of life and you will need to learn how to get better at failing. Yep, that's right, you need to learn how to get better at failing! That is, you will need to learn how to handle rejections, losses, defeats, and so on, and not let these failures destroy opportunities that may present in the future. One mistake that students and adults make is, when they fail, they give up on their dreams or goals. Remember this: You should never give up on what you love to do! No matter what happens to you and no matter how many times you are rejected, no matter how many times you fail, or no matter how many times you lose—you should never give up. Actually, the moment you give up on your dreams and goals because you did not succeed at that point is the moment that you fail.

Giving up equals failing! You must know that failure is a part of life, and if you don't know how to fail, you won't know how to succeed.

There are times when you move on and do other things, but this moving on process should be in response to refined ideas, not because you feel that you are inadequate or because you feel that you lack skills to meet goals.

Rap Music, Spoken Word, Performance Arts. One of the things that makes these groups fun and exciting is students can shape the groups based on their interests, talents, and passions. Within the group, students will have the opportunity to listen to rap music, write lyrics, create spoken word, record themselves (with their parents' permission), upload their performance on YouTube, and so on.

Over the years, I have jotted down my notes and thoughts, and have interviewed students about their experiences within these groups. I published this book based on my thoughts and the thoughts of students like you. After you read this book, I will consider your feedback along with the feedback from other students. Based on your feedback, I may re-write the book, based on what you and other students believe might be a more effective way of teaching SEL skills. I will do this because I think it is important to get the thoughts of students when creating programs and groups for them. Too often, teachers create programs and lessons based on what they believe might be fun and effective. In most cases, we are wrong and the lessons are beyond boring!

Social Emotional Learning Skills Are a Big Deal, Huh?

Based on the name of these skills—remember, they are *social emotional learning skills*—can you guess what they are about, or what they refer to?

The skills refer to learning how to manage yourself, including how to manage your emotions.

The main focus of this book will be on learning these skills, and here is why I know you will embrace this book: I will teach these skills

21

by referring to rap music and include discussions that pertain to hip-hop culture. I will use hip-hop because more and more youth are embracing this culture. I will use an array of strategies to teach SEL skills, but I will place emphases on rap music.

> *A fact about me: I am a fan of hip-hop as well!*
> *What school psychologist do you know who listens to rap music?*
> *Say word . . . Word. Cool!*
> *(Okay, I listen to rap music but don't say "word!")*

I will use the letters, "SEL" to refer to social emotional learning so that you do not have to keep reading *social emotional learning* throughout the book. For example, if you were explaining this book to your parents or friends, would you rather say the book is about "social emotional learning" every time you referred to these skills, or would you rather say "social emotional learning" only *one* time, and then simply say "SEL" after explaining the skills? I don't know about you, but I'd rather explain social emotional learning one time, and then say SEL when talking with people who know what SEL skills are.

My Promise to You

If you read this entire book, and work with your building or organization leader (for example, talk with your principal or organization leader) on how to create hip-hop SEL groups in your building, you will be able to do a host of things that you would not have been able to do if you had not participated in these groups, or read this book.

I will make you a promise—and you know what they say: You should never make a promise because, well, you never know what might happen that may interfere with keeping your promise. But I will make the promise anyway. I will promise because I am just that confident that you will enjoy this book, and that the book will change the way you view your life.

Are You Ready For the Promise?

Drum roll, please . . .
All right, here we go—

I promise that, if you read this entire book, and apply the SEL principles that I share within this book, you will
- gain the skills needed to reach achievable goals,
- increase confidence in your abilities,
- enhance your motivation to do well as a youth and student,
- increase your desire to do something worthwhile,
- improve your ability to manage your emotions—and more!

One last thing before we move on to the next chapter. You should know that simply reading this book will not take you from where you currently are to where you would like to be with meeting your goals. Rather, reading this book, applying the principles, and working with your teacher, school psychologist, social worker, or someone you have a relationship with will help you meet the goals that you create from this book.

There Is a First Time for Every Experience

There is something I think you should know: This is the first time I have written a book for youth—for young people like you and your peers. Since this is my first time doing this, I'll ask that you take it easy on me as you are reading this book. "Take it easy on me" means to give this book a shot and know that this is my first time writing a book in which I am speaking directly to teenagers. You should also know that I am very excited about this book and excited about the possibility of hearing from you via email! (You can find me at Dwayne@tier1education.com.)

I promise I will include things in this book that you can relate to—things such as hip-hop music, writing poetry, relationships, successes, and failures. The fact that I write about successes and failures ensures that you will relate to the book in some way. Everyone will experience success in some area of life and will experience failure in other areas. No one is ever successful in everything that they do; likewise, no one ever fails at everything that they do. We all experience success and failures in our lives.

How Do You Feel About School?

Have you ever felt bored to death by the way instruction is presented in school? I ask you this question because I meet with many students who tell me that they do not enjoy school because school is extremely boring.

Have You Ever Felt This Way?

Students have told me that they rarely learn in ways that are fun and entertaining. They have also told me that they rarely read and learn about things that are relevant to their experiences. Do you agree or disagree with these students? If you agree with them, then I would love to work with you. That's right, I want to work with you!

Let's Partner and Come Up With a Plan

My goal is to change the way instruction is provided to all students, including students of color and students who believe they do not enjoy school. You will be able to help me with this goal if you agree to work with me. You will have the chance to agree in Chapter 6.

My goal is to help students become extremely passionate about learning—and I will need your help. Often, educators create ideas and plans about how to teach you and your friends, but we rarely get your thoughts about how to make instruction interesting, relevant, and entertaining. When I say *relevant* I mean making instruction meaningful to *you*, based on *your* interests, passions, race, gender, and culture.

I want to use this book to show you and your peers that school does not have to be boring and mundane, and if you could help me with this, we could change the game in education. We could make learning fun for students who believe it is boring, help more students apply themselves at a deeper level, and help them prepare for life after high school.

Summary

Imagine that you have the opportunity to create hip-hop groups and programs where you and your friends could listen to rap music while learning how to build self-confidence and manage your emotions. Not only will you all listen to rap music in these groups, but also, you will have opportunities to write lyrics (if you are interested in writing), write spoken word, poetry, and engage in performance art. In addition, you all will have the opportunity to record yourselves and upload your videos on YouTube.

Does this sound exciting? In this book, I explain how you could create hip-hop groups at your school or organization, and how you could co-lead the groups with a staff member within your building.

What's Next?

In the next chapter, I will share with you a story about one of my students. For the purpose of this story, I will call him Bobby. Bobby was like most academically unmotivated students. He hated school and couldn't wait to graduate so that he would be done with school. Do you ever feel this way? I'll be honest and say that, when I met with Bobby and listened to his story, I was moved to tears! Be sure to read Bobby's story to see if you could relate to how he felt.

CHAPTER 2: "I HATE SCHOOL": THE STORY OF BOBBY

We make a living by what we get; we make a life by what we give.
—Winston Churchill

As a school psychologist, I have the privilege of working with a variety of students—from students who are extremely motivated academically and love school, to those who are extremely unmotivated academically and express their disdain for school. One of the best things about working as a school psychologist is helping students create a better life and future for themselves. Thus, I have embraced Winston Churchill's quote and it is one of my mottos. I have dedicated my life to giving to others; I truly believe that we make a life by what we give.

In this chapter, I share a story about what happens when we give to others; the story is about one of my students who hated school. I'll call my student "Bobby." As you read this chapter, place yourself in the story. Think about these two questions:

- Can I relate to Bobby?
- Do I have friends who are similar to Bobby?

If you can relate to Bobby, think about how you two are similar. If you have friends who are similar to Bobby, think about these students. What are their names? How are they similar?

The Story of Bobby

Bobby was a 16-year-old male. He was very likeable and respectful, but extremely unmotivated. When the bell rang to start class, Bobby would walk slowly in the hallways. In fact, he was often the only student in the hallway after the bell rang.

When I would see him, I would call his name, "Bobby . . . Bobby. Come here, man! You are walking as slow as you could, huh? You are walking like you don't have anywhere to be!" Every time I would see Bobby, I would say this to him. To this statement, he would smile and say, "Nope—I ain't got nowhere to be, Mr. Williams!" He'd then laugh and give me dap.

My office was located next to the dean's office in our school so students had to pass my office to get to their dean. Because of how our offices were arranged, I would see all of the students who had to go see their dean because of referrals. And I bet you could guess who I saw most. Yep—Bobby! Bobby was often in the dean's office because he rarely went to class. He would often roam the building or sit in the cafeteria during his class periods.

One day I invited Bobby to come talk with me in my office. I wanted to see if I could motivate him to start going to class. When I met with Bobby, we had small talk about his life, his family, who he lived with, his father, and other things. During our talk, we listened to music; Bobby would make comments about the music I listened to. He would often say, "My momma listens to this song all the time!" I would have R&B music playing in the background as I often listen to music while working. After small talk with Bobby, I got down to business. I began to talk about his many referrals and his tendency to skip class or come to class well after the bell rang. Although I do not remember our entire conversation, I remember talking about why he didn't believe he would be successful in school.

As Bobby rocked in his seat to the music that beat out of my phone, I asked him these questions. "What are your thoughts about your future? Do you plan to go to college?" I reminded Bobby that he would be graduating in two years and that these years would fly by. Bobby's response has stuck with me since the time he shared it. He explained, "You know, Mr. Williams, I am not sure if I will go to college. I think college would be fun and all, but nobody in my family went to college."

After telling me about why he didn't think he had a good chance at going to college, I asked him if he would be interested in joining my group, which was held during the school day. Our group was an academic motivational group; my purpose for creating the group was to boost academic motivation among students and to help them find hope in themselves.

Here is what he said about joining my group: "Mr. Williams, Imma [I'm going to] keep it all the way 100. . . . I get tired of y'all teachers talking to me about college and doing well in school. I bet none of y'all experienced what I experienced as a kid and teenager. I experienced all kinds of stuff. . . . I was even homeless at one point."

Here is what he said that made me emotional.

"It would be cool to work with somebody whose parents didn't graduate from college; I want to work with someone who hated school how I hate school; I want to work with someone who could understand what I mean when I say I can't wait to graduate—not to go to college, but to be done with school!"

He continued.

"All of y'all had it easy. Y'all have y'all's degree, y'all's parents graduated from college, put y'all through college, came from good families, and all of that. Y'all want us to do what y'all did, but y'all didn't experience what we experience."

As he spoke, I sat in my chair and listened attentively. He had my ear! When he finished talking, I looked at him, with watery eyes, and just kept saying, "Wow!" I literally said "wow" about five or six times before saying anything else. I then asked him if I could write down what he had said. I wanted to record his feedback because it was extremely powerful and emotional.

29

Why do you think I became emotional?

His feedback brought back memories of how I thought and felt when I was his age. From his feedback, I felt all kinds of emotions shoot through my body.

I became emotional because, although he didn't know it, I was very similar to him when I was his age. I experienced many of the things he talked about and more. In fact, my upbringing was worse than how he described his. After recording his responses, I went on to share my story with him; I also showed him a few newspaper articles of when I played football in high school. The articles that I showed him were published around 1998 and 1999 around the year I received a lot of attention as a running back for Dundee Crown High School. Back then I rushed for over 200 yards during football games and received many letters from colleges to attend their school to play football for their team.

In one of the newspaper articles, the editor talked about my difficulties with making good choices in school. The article revealed a story of when I spilled Kool-Aid® from my cup on a student in the cafeteria. Although I apologized about the spill, I eventually got into a fight with the student. This fight caused me to miss a county track meet that I was looking forward to competing in.

During this meeting with Bobby, I didn't even scratch the surface of how bad my experiences were as a teenager. It wasn't until later that I learned I needed to fully disclose my own past if I wanted students to trust me enough to disclose theirs.

I eventually shared my past with Bobby. As I shared my story with him—the story that I will share with you in the next chapter—he became increasingly attentive. In response to my story, he gave me dap and said, "I would have never imagined that you went through some of the same things I experienced! I initially said that I would prefer to work with someone who experienced things that I experienced. I guess I am talking with that person. And yeah . . . I would love to be a part of your group. When does it start?"

Bobby attended the group, was very engaged, led many of the sessions, and went on to graduate from high school. Not only did he graduate, but also he applied to college and attended a community college after high school, just as I did. He followed my steps toward achieving a college degree!

Summary

In this chapter, I shared the story of Bobby. Bobby was a very unmotivated student who would often skip class or come to class after the bell rang. Bobby explained to me that he was tired of teachers encouraging him to go to college. He explained that teachers had it easy in life, that they already had their degrees, completed school, and that their parents attended and graduated from college. He explained that he wanted to work with someone who experienced things that he experienced as a student, like being homeless and hating school. After sharing my story with Bobby, he was willing to work with me, as my story was very similar to his, and actually, even worse. Bobby allowed me to work with him and he went on to graduate from high school. Not only did he graduate, but also, he attended a community college, just as I did!

What's Next?

In the next chapter, I will share with you my story, the story that inspired Bobby to work with me and to help him navigate through the schooling process. As you read my story, think about yourself. Ask yourself if you can relate to my story. If you can't relate, then think of others who may have had similar experiences as me. Talk with your parents about my story and ask them if they experienced anything like I experienced growing up.

CHAPTER 3: PROJECT KIDS

Depending on the story that you're telling, you can be relatable to every-body or nobody. I try and tell everybody's story.
—Chance the Rapper

Have you ever thought about writing a book or writing music about your life? If you were to write a story about your life, consider the following questions.

- What would be the title?
- What would the book be about?
- Would it be a success story from start to finish?
- Would it start out with a personal struggle and end with conquering that struggle?
- Do you believe your story is worth telling?
- Do you believe, if you wrote a book about your life, people would read it?

Most stories start in a neutral state and by the middle of the story, something goes awry; by the end of the story, there is a life lesson.

People all over the world are making money and changing lives by telling their story. Think about your favorite rappers. I would bet that in some of their songs they share their story. In this chapter I will share with you my story, the story that encouraged Bobby tremendously and helped him find hope.

It is important that you read the previous chapter prior to reading this one. I want you to read the previous chapter because it sets the tone for this chapter; also, I want you to read the story of Bobby to see if you can relate to him.

Bobby hated school and prior to my working with him, he explained that he would like to work with a counselor who understood his struggle. After sharing my story with Bobby, he was excited to work with me, and I helped him finish his last two years of high school strong. Even more, he went on to college to pursue a career!

My story was a huge factor in encouraging Bobby to work with me. It showed him that he could relate to me in many ways. Because my story was so successful at encouraging him, I will share my story with you. And trust me when I say that you would never imagine what I experienced growing up.

Your Story Is Worth a Million Bucks!

As an author, I enjoy reading and writing about success stories of students. Perhaps your story will be in the second edition of this book. Wouldn't that be super cool to read your story in a published book? In order to have your story placed in a book that I write, it will have to be about overcoming something that was stressful or difficult, something similar to Bobby's story. It will have to be a success story. In fact, if you think you want to have your story placed in one of my books, be sure to shoot me an email and explain why you think your story should be in my books. Also, if you would like to write a book about your life, but don't know where to start, email me. I may be able to help you get started!

In this chapter, I will share my story, a story of a young Black boy who

- grew up in poverty,
- lived in housing projects,
- was retained in the first grade because he could not read,
- struggled with math,
- graduated from high school with a 1-point something GPA,

- obtained an ACT composite score of 15—and failed miserably on all standardized tests he ever took from elementary through high school.

I will talk about my experiences living in poverty and how I hated school as a student. I will talk about how I got into fights in high school and made poor decisions. More importantly, I discuss how, although I lived in poverty and hated school, I eventually graduated and enrolled in various colleges, where I earned an associate's degree (AA) in liberal arts from William Rainey Harper Community College, a bachelor's degree in psychology (BA) from Fairmont State University, a master's degree in psychology (MA) from Marshall University Graduate College, and an Educational Specialist degree (EdS) from Marshall University Graduate College.

In addition to earning many degrees, I am the owner of a business and also an author of four books. How did a Black boy who lived in poverty and in the projects experience such success? How did he become successful in that he learned to make a ton of money and become an entrepreneur, published author, and professional speaker? I will answer these questions, and in the next few chapters, I will discuss how you could do exactly what you want to do in life, no matter how your grades may look at the present moment. Okay—are you ready for this story? Cool, here we go . . .

The Projects

I was raised in the projects, roaches and rats,
smokers out back selling their momma's sofa . . .
—Jay Z

Not all students grow up in communities where things are all good. Some students grow up in neighborhoods where there are very few resources, in terms of money for food, clothes, and daily necessities. The Projects, short for housing projects, is one example of these communities.

Many rappers talk about the housing projects they grew up in, or projects that are within their city. For example Jay Z talks about Marcie Projects and Nas talks about Queensbridge. In this chapter, I will talk about the John Hay Homes, the projects where my family and I lived for part of my early childhood years.

John Hay Homes

When I was two years old, my parents separated. Prior to their separation, my family—father, mother, brother and sister—lived in a suburb northwest of Chicago. My parents did not graduate from high school. In fact, my mother dropped out of school as a junior and my father dropped out as a sophomore. Although my parents eventually went back to school to earn their diplomas when they were in their 40s, their dropping out of school determined the kind of life I would live as a kid.

When they separated, my mother and I moved to Springfield, Illinois, along with my older brother and sister. Springfield was an ideal place to move because my aunts, uncles, cousins, grandmother, and grandfather lived there. This was my family on my mother's side.

Because my mother did not graduate from high school, she had very few opportunities as a young parent. In fact, her opportunities and resources were so limited that our family relied on the government for support. My mother received assistance from the government in the form of food stamps and vouchers for food to support my siblings and me. In addition to receiving food stamps, our family lived in the John Hay Homes Housing Projects, where most students lived whose parents dropped out of school and relied on the government for support.

Where Were the Fathers and Grandfathers?

The majority of the residents who lived in these projects were Black. Usually, the fathers were not around—or at least did not live in the homes with their children—which meant the mothers headed the homes. Actually, I do not remember seeing the fathers of my friends; I surely never met them. I would usually see my friends' mothers, aunts, uncles, and grandmothers. I do not recall seeing their fathers or grandfathers, or even hearing my friends talk about them when we conversed.

The housing projects were horrible and decrepit. The apartments were infected with all sorts of bugs. For example, roaches occupied every space in the apartments and gigantic water bugs lounged directly outside the front doors, as if they waited patiently for residents to return home. Roaches were so prevalent that they were in drawers, cabinets, bathtubs, peanut butter, jelly, bread, and other foods. Of course, when we noticed the roaches in food we would trash whatever food it was. It was always depressing to find bugs in cereal boxes and other foods because we didn't have much to eat to begin with.

The projects were a filthy living space for anyone to occupy. But because of limited resources, my mother could not afford to move into anything better than the projects. Not only did my immediate family live here, but also my grandmother, aunts, uncles, and cousins lived in the projects, blocks away from our apartment. Although these living conditions were horrid, I was used to them. It was normal to come home to a house full of roaches crawling across countertops and see them scamper across the refrigerator and floor once someone turned the lights on.

I was used to getting food stamps as allowance and enjoyed walking to the penny candy store with my siblings and cousins to buy penny candy from Mr. Chester, an old White man who owned a candy store near the 'hood. Chester was popular among poor kids living in the projects because he accepted food stamps and was kind to us all.

At home we earned food stamps for every good deed that we did. In fact, my grandmother still owes me a dollar food stamp for sweeping the backroom of her house. During the early '80s my grandmother said she would give me a dollar food stamp if I swept her room. I usually jumped at every opportunity to earn a food stamp. I rushed to find a broom and cleaned the back room to the point it was spotless. She acknowledged my work but never gave me the food stamp that she had promised. When I visit my family in Springfield, Illinois, and meet with my grandmother, I ask her this question: "Do you still have the food stamp that you owe me!" In response, she says, "Dwayne, I do still owe you that food stamp, don't I?!" She and I usually laugh at these cherished memories as we reach to give each other a hug.

The Life of a Kid Living in Poverty

Although my family lived in the projects, lived off food stamps, and received other free resources from the government, I had no idea that my family and I lived in poverty. After all, we rarely left the projects and so we were not exposed to any other kind of life. We didn't have anything to which we could compare these living conditions.

The young boys in the projects played freeze tag, flipped against each other (backflip competitions), raced, and played at the park. The young girls played single and double-dutch, hop scotch, and drew on the sidewalks with colorful crayons. Within the projects, there was this place called the Center.

We would go to the Center where staff members created opportunities for kids to create crafts and other things. The Center also had trampolines where we all enjoyed trying to do "Double-No's" in the air. If you flip, or are in gymnastics, you know what I mean by *double-no's*; double-no's are when you jump in the air high enough to flip twice before returning to the ground. "No's" stand for "no hands," in that when you flipped, you would flip without touching the ground with your hands.

We also went to this place the kids in the 'hood called, the Green Building. We called it that because it was green. We didn't put a lot of thought into the name. The Green Building was kind of like the Center. But the Green Building was where kids ate breakfast and lunch. Also, staff members would lay mats outside for community kids to flip on. We also played air hockey at the Green Building and the Center.

While the young kids stayed busy playing freeze tag, flipping, and chasing each other around the parks, the Green Building, and the Center, the teenage boys and girls would play this game called "Hide and Go Get it." The game sounded fun. I had no idea what they were hiding and going to get, but the game usually started by someone asking this question: "Y'all want to play hide and go get it?" I was too young to understand this game. The adults in the hood would call the teenagers who played "hide and go get it" mannish. I had no idea what they meant by "so-and-so . . . with his mannish tail!" until I became a teenager. When I found out what the teenagers were hiding and going to get, I also called them mannish, just as the adults did.

Flipping in the Ghetto on a Dirty Mattress!

I attended Lincoln Elementary School, located blocks away from the projects, in Springfield, Illinois. I was popular among my friends because I was one of the fastest students my age and was the "coldest one at flipping." Being "cold" at something simply meant that you were really good at whatever you were cold at. So being cold at flipping meant that I was one of the best at doing backflips.

Surprisingly, I actually hear students use the word *cold* today just as we used it when I was a kid!

I was cold at doing backflips because that is what we did in the projects every day. We would drag dirty, used mattresses we found in the projects and flip on them. Residents would throw their mattresses outside and kids would drag them around the projects. How nasty does that sound? We would also go to the second floor of the apartments, open the window, and take turns flipping out, onto the mattresses. The drop was about 18 feet! We were project kids, and fearless. Apparently, flipping on dirty mattresses was common in the hood. In her song, the "Miseducation of Lauryn Hill," Lauryn also comments about her experiences with flipping in the ghetto on a dirty mattress.

My friends, brother, sister, and I would skip school to have backflip contests, although my sister did not flip as we did; she was usually in the house controlling the music from the living room. We would leave for school early in the morning, but when our mothers left for work, we would return to the house and have flip parties.

Flip parties were parties that we had in which friends came over; we blasted music and competed against one another doing backflips. I usually shut the parties down by doing multiple "no's" and twists within one routine. I would also run toward a wall, jump in the air, and while in the air kick the wall and then flip backward. Not too many of my friends could do this. I would do this against buildings, trees, poles, or anything that would not move when I kicked it.

Elementary School

By the end of first grade, my mother received horrible news. The principal at Lincoln Elementary School contacted her and recommended that she come in for a meeting. When she went, she took me, and the two of us met with my teacher and principal.

During this meeting, my mother was informed that I would be retained—held back—because I could not read. Although all of my friends who I flipped with and raced against advanced to second grade, I had to return to first grade because I couldn't read.

Why do you believe reading was so difficult for me?

This news was horrible and depressing. I could not read because I did not practice reading within my home. I had no one to help me read after school because my mother worked multiple jobs to support our family. Instead of reading, I played the Coleco Vision and Atari—video games that are comparable, in some ways, to the Xbox and PlayStation nowadays. The reality was I needed more practice than I received during the school hours. Can you think of something that you might be struggling with only because you do not study? What I have learned in life is that the things that are difficult for us are those things we do not practice daily.

I Hated School . . . But Loved Sports!

I eventually learned how to read, but hated school with a passion. In fact, I disliked school so much that I rarely applied myself during elementary, middle, or high school. Because I was amazingly athletic, I played sports in school, which is really the only reason I was excited about attending.

Middle School

My first attempt at playing football was in middle school. I joined a team called the "Junior Chargers." I often tell a funny story about football and my football helmet. Well, it is interesting to share now, but back in the day, it was not as funny. Throughout my elementary and middle school years, we were often homeless. One time, when we became homeless, my mother, brother, sister, and I were walking the streets. My brother and sister packed a huge bag in which they stored their valuables. I do not recall what my mom brought along with her, but for me, I brought my football helmet. That was it. While my brother and sister dragged their bags up and down the dark roads, I grasped tightly the facemask of my white and blue Junior Chargers football helmet. During this time in my life, we often stayed with friends and church members. At one point, my family lived in the Holiday Inn.

Living in the hotel was kind of cool because after school we would rush to take our backpacks to our hotel room and dash downstairs to the swimming pool to swim. We did this so often that now when I smell chlorine, it reminds me of the days we were homeless and lived in the Holiday Inn, in Elgin, Illinois.

During middle school I got into fights. One funny story is, one time when I got into a fight in 6th grade, I was sent to the office. The principal attempted to call my mother, but she couldn't pick me up right away because she was working. So the principal flipped through the contact form and read aloud my emergency contact's name, Sister Reed. As he read her name, he scratched his head and said, "Hhmmm . . . Sister Reed! Is your emergency contact a nun?" I thought this was hilarious. I busted out laughing! At this point, I taught him all about our church culture way of calling each other Brother So-and–so and Sister So-and-so. We called all the adults "brother" and "sister" in our church; an example would be Sister Outlaw or Brother Reed. Eventually, I was able to graduate from 8th grade and transition to high school.

High School

In high school, I was required to take the lowest math classes offered for my grade. Even with these low classes, I failed some of them, and the ones I passed, I did so with low Ds and Cs. In addition to performing poorly academically, I got into many fights in school. In fact I got into so many fights that I had to miss many track meets and football games because of suspensions.

In one incident, I was in the lunchroom and was walking and carrying a tray that held a cup of Kool-Aid® I had planned to have with my lunch. As I walked to my seat, I accidentally spilled the Kool-Aid®

on another student's white t-shirt, and this incident caused a fight to break out! During the fight, the students in the cafeteria went nuts! They screamed, jumped over tables, threw food, and ran around like wild animals.

I was suspended for this fight and had to miss the county state track meet, which was a popular track meet that I was looking forward to competing in. I graduated from high school, but because of an ACT score of 15 and because my GPA was 1-point something, I had to take remedial classes when I entered college, which caused me to waste a lot of money on courses that I did not get credit for.

College Life

I attended a well-known university, where I planned to play football. I had to sit out a year because of my low GPA and poor ACT score. While at this university, the running back coach had this rule that running backs could not practice with earrings in their ears. I had three holes in my ear and wore three expensive diamond studs. Well, one day, I forgot to take my earrings out, and I came out to practice, at which point the running back coach blasted me! He screamed at me for the earrings, swore at me, and verbally chastised me. In response, I swore back at the coach, and we exchanged swear words. In the end, the coached won. He shouted, "Go get your shit and get the hell out of here!"

At this point, I left practice, went back to my dorm, packed my things up and prepared to leave college. I left this university and went to a community college named William Rainey Harper College—commonly known as Harper Community College, in Palatine, Illinois, a northwest suburb of Chicago.

While at Harper College, I continued to hate school. I would skip class, and when I was in class, I would sleep. I did so horribly at the community college that I was on probation because of my GPA, and I received a letter from the college stating that I would not be eligible for financial aid if I did not bring my grades up. It was common practice for football players to skip class and play cards; while skipping class, we played cards—Spades to be exact. We would play cards for hours! Actually we played cards from the time we met in the morning until practice started in the afternoon.

While at Harper College, I met a friend who eventually became my girlfriend. My girlfriend helped me out tremendously. She was the kind of college student who had goals and knew exactly what she wanted out of life. In fact, while I was in the hallways playing cards with other football players and skipping class, she would study for hours in the library down the hall from where we played.

In her attempt to help me bring my grades up, she completed a couple math tests and wrote a few papers for me. Although I was happy that she completed my math tests, this came back to haunt me. I was horrible at math and shied away from things that pertained to calculating and problem solving using numbers. In the end, getting her to complete my math tests was not the best idea.

One of the best things she did for me was have a conversation about why she thought I should study psychology. She explained that she could tell there was not much that I wanted to study while at Harper and that I was academically unmotivated; after all, I had taken and failed many business, economics, and management courses, which resulted in my low GPA. She also reminded me of the fact that if I did not make changes in my behaviors as a college student, my financial aid would be taken away.

She recommended that I study psychology; she felt that it was something I would enjoy. Considering there was nothing that I was interested in studying, I thought about it. Her recommendation changed my life! Although I failed the Introduction to Psychology 101 class—the very basic psychology course offered—I eventually stuck with psychology, earned a bachelor and master degree in it, and eventually earned a degree that now allows me to practice as a school psychologist!

I was a running back for Harper's football team. I was good enough to earn a scholarship to a Division II school. When I found out about the scholarship opportunity, I called the college coaches and scheduled a visit to the university. I remember buying a bus ticket, and riding the bus for 17 hours to Fairmont, West Virginia. This bus ride was excruciating! I remember arriving in Fairmont as if it was yesterday. The bus I rode eventually stopped, and the driver said, "Welcome to Fairmont, West Virginia!" When I heard this, I woke up, pulled my pick out of my pocket, and picked my curly, mini Afro. I used to put chemicals in my hair to make it curly.

I used products like S-Curls, Pro-line, and Duke. Have you ever heard of these products? The next time you go to a hair supply store, or Wal-Mart, ask them if they sell these items. If they do, check them out. Check out the pictures of the hairstyles on the box covers, and read the back of the box. I am sure you will laugh at what I used to do to my hair. My wife tells me that she believes I am bald today because of these products. I thought I was cool though, and as Kanye West said, couldn't nobody tell me nothing!

Fairmont State University

While at Fairmont University, where I would go on to earn my bachelor's degree, and play football, I became extremely fascinated about learning. This was weird because, remember, I hated school. What do you believe changed my thoughts and interests about school? The answer is my interest in psychology. I loved learning about why people dream, how people learn, what motivates people to demonstrate certain behaviors, and how the mind functions.

My love for psychology and learning resulted in my quitting the football team at Fairmont State University so that I would have more time to study psychology, bring my GPA up, and prepare for graduate school. I cannot explain how excited I became about learning and psychology. It was a new love that I had found. I loved reading about psychology to the extent that when my roommates would throw parties, I would be on the couch reading psychology books—all while a house full of young ladies danced around the house and mingled with the guys.

My love for psychology increased my interest to go to the university's library where I often studied psychology books for hours. There were times when I would go to the library around 3:00 PM, after my classes ended, and would not leave the library until it closed, around 11 or 12:00! I had found my love, and it was psychology. My GPA in the area of psychology was around 3.8; I usually outperformed my peers on psychology tests and quizzes. I found these tests to be easy, while other students found them to be difficult.

Perhaps the best thing about attending Fairmont State University was that I met a young lady there who was on the swim team. I would often see her as I went to football practice. The young lady was very quiet and kept to herself. I thought she was cute and wanted to get to know her, but never introduced myself to her. One day, as I waited outside for my class to start, I noticed her sitting in a chair, waiting for her class to start. When I noticed her, I felt the urge to go say something to her. I had no clue what to say because we had not met previously. But I had an idea! Someone told me that she attended church every Sunday, and so I thought it might be smooth to introduce myself to her, let her know that I was not from Fairmont, and tell her that I was wondering if there were any good churches around that I could check out. This idea worked! From this, she explained that her dad was a pastor and that I should check out the church she and her dad attended. We exchanged numbers and she explained that, if I wanted to go, to call her Saturday night or Sunday morning and she would pick me up. As I walked away, I told her that I would call to let her know about church, but that I also wanted to call her to get to know her a little better. My line worked. This young lady is now my wife and we have two beautiful children!

Marshall University

I eventually graduated from Fairmont State and attended Marshall University. While at Marshall, I did some cool things. It was at this time that I became unusually interested in writing. I talked with professors about how I disagreed with many textbooks that I read, and I wrote articles about students who come from impoverished backgrounds. Other students who were in my program seemed to believe everything they read from those books, but not me, for I lived in conditions that the books spoke about, and my experiences weren't similar to the way the books described them.

I felt a strong connection with students who lived in impoverished backgrounds. My connection came as a result of my experiences living in poverty, and my experiences living in the projects where we received government assistance. I felt that White authors and researchers from middle class backgrounds were talking and publishing articles about "impoverished parents and students," but had no clue what these people experienced on the regular. I felt I understood their struggle and that, although I was no longer a part of that community, I had to rep for them, and that is what I did.

I was thrilled to have gotten an article published during my second year as a graduate student, and this was a big deal because most graduate students were not publishing articles. The article that I wrote was published in a journal that usually published articles that were written by professors and scholars who held doctoral degrees. I wrote a paper explaining how I disagreed with the work of an author named Ruby Payne.

When you write a paper in response to someone else's work, in which you disagree with what the author says in the book or article, it is called a *rebuttal paper*. So I wrote a rebuttal paper in which I believed that her book was all about stereotypes. I felt that she stereotyped poor people, a group who are perhaps the most voiceless people in America.

In addition to all of this success, I won a $500 writing award in which I wrote a paper titled, "The Dark and Desolate Valley of Segregation: The Hidden Truth." In this paper, I wrote about how psychology programs talk about many European and White psychologists, but fail to talk about Black psychologists and other psychologists of color; I also talked about how textbooks rarely include the experiences and lives of Black people. This writing contest was offered at the university I attended, and there were many participants. My paper won first place, and I earned some extra cash and was awarded a plaque in front of hundreds of people.

Boy was I on a roll!

During my graduate level years, I mentored many of my school psychology students in research and writing, special education law, and statistics. I was literally frightened to take statistics because it is all about analyzing and working with numbers. I was afraid of this class because, remember, I was horrible at math. But guess what, I earned a 97%!

During my second year in graduate school, I got tired of hearing how poorly students of color perform compared to White students on IQ tests and other measures, and I began to do something about that as well. I began to study how to increase performance among students of color, primarily African American students.

I began to read articles on how Black students felt about their teachers and articles that explained the need to create learning activities that align with the lives and interests of Black students. Aligned with my interest, I conducted a study with 300 students, in which I got their feedback and perceptions of school.

After graduating, I landed a job as a school psychologist, where I worked with teachers to help increase motivation and performance among students in the classroom. I also began to apply all of the things I had learned in college about increasing performance among students of color; I studied the importance of culture in education for over five years and so I had a lot of ideas tucked away in my mind of what might work.

Because an array of administrators and teachers emailed me with requests to train their teachers on how to increase performance among students of color, I was inspired to start my own business, in which I helped districts create effective models for their students.

I began to grow a passion for writing and began writing education books. One of my most successful books is titled, *An RTI Guide to Improving Performance of African American Students*. Interestingly, I self-published this book, which means I was the actual publishing company. The self-published book received a tremendous amount of attention, and eventually, a well-known education publishing company offered to take on the book. The publishing company made it possible for my book to be available throughout the nation, and available in European countries.

In addition to the book's success, I made thousands and thousands of dollars training school districts on how to create programs and groups that are effective at increasing engagement and performance among students of color and students who come from culturally diverse backgrounds; one group that I train educators on is the hip-hop SEL program that I discuss in this book.

When I first got started, I made $30,000 doing presentations and trainings. To be exact, I made $30,000 by giving only 4 presentations! I worked a little over 30 hours, and this included preparing for presentations and actually giving the presentations. This is an average pay of about $1,000 an hour! This was a huge pay break for me considering the average college student who starts a job makes about $30,000 a year. That is right, a year! This means that I made in "thirty hours" what these graduates make in a full year. To put this in perspective, there are only 24 hours in one day. Students who graduate often make between $15 and $50 an hour, depending on their profession, compared to the $1,000 an hour that I made.

That's My Story . . .

That is a little about my background. I think in another book I will dedicate the entire book to telling my story. I do not have the space in this book to go into more detail. I like to share my story because students often believe that teachers did not experience difficult lives. Some teachers did not live in poverty and experience some of the things I did, while others have experiences similar to mine; some have even worse stories! I think it is interesting to tell my story because I work with students every day who remind me of how I was in school, students who demonstrate the same behaviors I demonstrated when I was a teenager. I am usually effective at working with these students because, often, I can empathize with them and understand their struggle.

Summary

When I was two years old, my father and mother separated. My dad lived in a northwest suburb of Chicago and my mother moved to Springfield, Illinois. My father dropped out of school when he was a sophomore and my mother dropped out when she was a junior. Because my mother dropped out of school, we depended on the welfare system for support and received food stamps, food vouchers, and lived in poverty. Because my mother worked so many hours in the evenings, I did not have much support with learning how to read. Consequently, I was held back in the first grade because of reading challenges.

I literally hated school and got into a lot of trouble during my middle and high school years. I graduated high school with a 1-point something GPA and obtained a composite ACT score of 15. I performed horribly on all state tests that I took. I experienced a change in my attitude when I started studying psychology. I would study for hours. During graduate school, I won a writing award and published an article. This was drastically different from my experiences as a student in kindergarten through 12th grade. Although I grew up in the projects and lived in poverty, I am now a published author and a leading consultant within the field of education! If you are interested, check out my business website at www.tier1education.com.

What's Next?

In the next chapter, I will share the secret of my success and explain how, no matter what your grades are now, and no matter what you have experienced in your life, you could also overcome your struggles and prepare to make big bucks, with a lucrative career!

CHAPTER 4: REFLECTING ON MY STORY

To read without reflecting is like eating without digesting.
—Edmund Burke

There you have it! You are now familiar with my story, which means you know more about me than most other people do. You spent the last chapter reading, perhaps nonstop, and so in this chapter, I want you to use your mind in a different way. I want you to actually *think* about what you read in the previous chapter; that is, think about my story. Often, we read books and when we complete a chapter, we move on to the next chapter, and then the next, and then the next, and so on, continuously, without actually stopping to reflect on what we read. That is what I want you to do in this chapter, to reflect on my story and to think about how life would be if you had to live as I did, in poverty—in the projects.

But before you do that, I want to introduce a word to you, a word that you may not have attempted to memorize before. Interestingly, I was in the process of teaching my students the definition of the word that I am about to teach you, and for some odd reason, one of my colleagues explained that they didn't think students could really understand and learn the word. My question to my colleagues was, "Why not? Why don't you think they could learn this term?" Learning is all about memory, and so if you could remember what I am about to say, then you can learn the word.

Okay—here we go!

The word that I am about to teach you explains why most people are successful. The word is *engagement*, and I will use it in a sentence:

"My hope is that this book will increase *engagement*
among the students who read it!"

I will use it in another sentence, in a different way:

"When people *engage*, they usually learn at a high level!"

Based on my sentences, what do you think the word *engagement* means?
Or what do you think it means to engage? Engagement means a lot of
different things, but based on the way we are using it, it means to apply
yourself. That is, to read, to write, to think about what is discussed,
to answer questions, and so on. So when you do these things—read,
write, and raise your hand to answer a question, you are engaged, or
you engage yourself.

Make sure you are paying attention because I am going somewhere
with this word. Also, I want you to *engage* yourself by reflecting on my
story.

There are at least three different ways we can engage ourselves (Fredricks, Blumenfeld, & Paris, 2004):

Behavioral Engagement: This simply means engaging by
"doing something" that pertains to an assignment or activity. Examples include raising your hand, asking a question,
answering a question, nodding your head to some idea, disagreeing with someone, writing, and so on.

Cognitive Engagement: This simply means you engage by
thinking about something on a deep level. Thinking about
my story is an example of cognitive engagement. The word
cognitive simply means "thinking," or "to think."

Affective Engagement: This is a kind of engagement in
which your feelings are involved. Whenever you do things
that are fun, and you feel good about what you are doing,
this is *affective engagement.* In my hip-hop groups, we used

music, wrote lyrics, and performed to increase affective engagement in our groups.

I defined these different ways that you could engage yourself because I will refer to them throughout this book. I will have you to engage in one of the above three ways. At this time, I want you to engage in *cognitive* and *behavioral* engagement. Again, *cognitive engagement* simply means to think; and so I want you to think about my story. *Behavioral engagement* usually involves moving your body in some way. When you move your hand and use your fingers to write, you are engaging behaviorally. And so, with this, I want you to think about my story (cognitive engagement) and to write down your thoughts (behavioral engagement) about my story.

I want you to think so deeply about my story that you could actually visualize a little Black boy growing up in the projects, failing first grade, getting into fights in middle and high school, being homeless, obtaining a 1-point something GPA, scoring extremely low on state standardized tests, including the ACT. But also, think deeply about all of the things this little Black boy was able to do in life, despite his struggles throughout his development.

As you think about my story, put yourself in my shoes. How is my story similar to or different from your story? I want you to write down your thoughts on the space below. Before you do that, I will give you another overview of the things I have accomplished, despite living in the projects and being a homeless student. These include the following:

- Graduated from college to earn an associate's degree, bachelor's degree, and two master's degrees;
- Wrote four books (at the time this book was published);
- Landed a contract with a top academic publishing company;
- Helped students learn to read and write effectively;
- Trained school districts on how to make instruction relevant to the lives of students of color as the CEO of an educational consulting business;

- Received requests to write books for professors and others (this is called *ghostwriting*);
- Spoke professionally to a variety of organizations in a variety of venues;
- Coached teachers, business owners, and others to reach goals and experience success in their lives.

Be Sure to Engage Yourself . . .

Are you ready to start processing my story? Okay cool! Here is what I want you to do.

- Turn to Chapter 3 and quickly scan my story.
- Underline anything you believe is interesting, relevant to you or someone you know, including family members and/or friends.
- Skim my experiences in elementary, middle, and high school—and compare these to your experiences as a student.
- Think about people you know who struggle in school like I did. Do you think they might be able to accomplish the things I have accomplished—such as writing a book, starting a business, and so on?
- Put yourself in my shoes. How would you have coped with the things I experienced?
- How do you relate to my story? How is it relevant to you or someone you know?

If you had read my accomplishments, without knowing about my struggles, would you have assumed that I grew up in the projects and disliked school? Or that I came from parents who graduated from college?

Does my story inspire you? If so, in what way? Does it give you hope?

Share my accomplishments with your teachers, friends, and family members. Tell them all of the things I have accomplished in life.

For example, you could say, the author of the book that I am reading earned two master's degrees, started his own business, has published four books, is a success coach, and is a school psychologist. Based on his accomplishments, how do you think he was as a student in elementary, middle, and high school? Do you think he was an A-student, B-student, C-student, D- student? You could come up with your own questions similar to the one you just read.

DO NOT tell them about my life as a child—about growing up in the projects, being homeless, living in poverty, and disliking school. After you tell them about all of my accomplishments, ask them how they think my childhood was. After they guess, you should share my struggles with them.

Don't let them say, "I don't know," or "I have no idea" how he was. If they say that, just say, "Take a guess. . . . He has multiple degrees, is an author, started his own business, and so on." Write their responses in the spaces below. I want you to do this to see how people think about success. Sometimes people think that success is given—that people become successful by getting things handed to them—rather than earning things. When you ask your friends, teachers, and family member, I want you to include their thoughts on the space below, based on the person you ask. Put your friend's response in the space where it says "friend's response." Do the same for your teacher and family member.

Friend's response: _____

Teacher's response: _____

Family member's response: _____

57

Summary

When I ran my hip-hop SEL group, a few of my colleagues asked me why I was teaching my students the definition of the word *engagement*. The colleagues explained that they didn't believe my students would be able to learn what the word means. To engage simply means to apply yourself. If you want to become a rapper, then how could you engage yourself? The answer is you could engage yourself behaviorally (by watching people rap, observing them, and so on), you could engage cognitively (by thinking about rap songs, thinking about the lyrics you heard, and thinking about how to develop your talent), or you could engage yourself affectively (by doing some activity that you love, an activity that pertains to rapping that will send positive emotions throughout your body). Likewise, if you want to become a good writer, then you have to engage yourself. Whatever you do, you will have to engage yourself; that is, you will have to apply yourself and practice. In this chapter, I asked that you engage yourself by thinking about my story and reflecting on how it would be to live a life in poverty as I did when I was a kid.

What's Next?

In the next chapter, I will share with you the main reasons why I struggled in school and the method I used to bounce back. I will explain how you could use my method to create whatever kind of life you'd like to live.

CHAPTER 5: NO PRACTICE, NO PROGRESS

Practice makes progress . . .
—unknown author

Hopefully, prior to getting to this chapter, you have read my story in Chapter 3 and completed the writing assignment. In this chapter, I want to share with you why I failed continuously in school. I would bet all the money that I have that my reason for failing in school is the same reason—or one reason—you have failed at something in your life.

I bet you could guess why I failed. It's not rocket science. It is not because my parents dropped out of high school, either; it is not because of poverty, or because we lived in the projects. The reason I failed is because I did not apply myself; I did not practice. I attended school, listened while in class, but when I got home, I did nothing. Well, actually, that is a lie. I played the Coleco Vision, Atari, and ran around the neighborhood, playing with friends and flipping in the community.

Here is the deal. We'll be good at the things we practice daily.

No practice—no progress!

I flipped on the regular, and there weren't too many kids—my age or older—who could touch me when it came to flipping. As explained earlier, I would practice "full twists" and other complicated flips. I practiced until I could do these with ease. In fact, I practiced doing full twists so often that when I jumped in the air to do a "no" (no-hand back flip), or half twist, I would automatically do a full twist. My body would twist automatically. I had to "un-train" myself from automatically doing full twists.

I also explained that I would run toward a brick wall, or a tree, jump in the air, and while in the air, kick against the wall or tree and flip backwards. I would try other complicated flips as well. I perfected flipping and would always win when I competed against my peers. Actually, there were only two people in the hood who were better than me. These two people were amazingly talented when it came to flipping. They could do things that I couldn't do, or if I could do the things they did, they just made it look better.

That is my story.

I failed because I did not apply myself—not because I was unintelligent, stupid, or lacked sense. I was unable to read in first grade and so I was held back. When the decision was made to hold me back, my teacher did not sprinkle pixie dust on me or do some magical stunt the following year to get me to learn how to read. Rather, I just started reading more. I practiced. Period. There is no magic to how we learn.

We learn by doing. In fact, I am sure you could learn just about whatever you want to learn if you believe in yourself and practice long enough to learn the skills—whether these are math, reading, or writing skills. If you want to get better in a particular area of life, then you have to learn skills that will help you get better, and you have to practice these skills daily. The reason that many of us fail and do not achieve goals is because we do not work hard enough.

I could not write grammatically correct sentences until I entered college. Trust me when I said I wrote extremely poorly. The reason I could not write grammatically correct sentences is because I spoke Black Vernacular English only; I was unable to code-switch. *Code-switching* is being able to speak one way, then switch it up and speak another way. For example, usually, when you are with your friends, you may speak a certain way and use certain words. You may say your words in ways that only your friends can understand. But in the classroom, you are usually required to write and speak Standard English. If you are able to speak the way you speak around your friends and switch it up in the classroom, and speak and write Standard English, then you are able to code-switch. Code-switching is an important skill to master.

No one around me taught me how to code-switch, to convert the way I spoke—which is often called Black Vernacular English—to Standard English.

I took several English courses, but again, I did not apply myself. I would just get Fs on my papers and writing assignments, and that was that. It is important to note that taking English courses and teaching students how to code-switch are two different kinds of teaching. No one really sat me down to explain the difference between Black Vernacular English and Standard English—so I went on writing and speaking the way I spoke since living in the projects, as everyone in my community spoke and wrote. No one was able to code-switch in my community—that is, able to use both Black Vernacular English and Standard English. They just didn't have the skills.

Practicing and applying ourselves is critical, and if we do not practice the things that we learn, we will never learn how to apply those things.

Point Blank. Period!

It is what it is. There is no other way I could explain this. If you do not practice, you will not learn. Now check this out. I went from being unable to read, obtaining 1-point something GPA in high school, scoring extremely low on my state tests, to earning a 3.8 in my psychology studies and a 4.0 in both of my graduate programs, to writing books, to tutoring my graduate level peers in the areas of research and writing and statistics, to being asked to edit journals as a graduate student. Isn't this amazing! I also get emails from professors requesting that I coach them through the process of writing books. Professors also ask me to ghostwrite for them—that is, they pay me money to write for them. But when I write, I do not identify myself as the author. That is what ghostwriting is.

I say all of this to say that, once I became excited about education, psychology, and school psychology, I began to apply myself. Once I applied myself, I began to do things I never thought I'd be able to do.

The Most Common Myth

Think about the students you know who get good grades and receive just about all As. Bring these students to your mind. Who are they? What do they look like? Now, why do you think they get As? Do you think they were born as super smart babies? No! I will say it again. No! No! No!

We become skillful by interacting with the things in our environments—by reading books, writing ideas and thinking about those ideas, studying, and getting help with the things we do not understand. This is how we become skillful in anything that we do, whether it's backflipping or writing books.

Let's use my story as an example. I did horribly in school because I did not practice, read, write, or apply myself inside or outside of school. The result: I could not read, my GPA was 1-point something, my ACT score was 15, and the list goes on. Once I set my mind to being a successful student, I began to make transitions in how I approached learning. I began to study.

From training my mind to process information (that is, to think about and reason about information), I can write a book in a week! Of course this depends on the number of words or pages, but I could write a short book within a week's time. The reason I can write a book is not because I was born very smart. I wasn't. I can write books because I know a lot of information about the things I write about. I could sit at a computer and write for days about the content of my books. I'll give you a perfect example: As I am writing this book, I am typing away, non-stop. In fact, I finished this book within a month or so!

Here is the deal. Reading does many things to your mind.

It helps you become a better writer, in that you are able to see, from reading books, examples of what good writing is; reading exposes you to appropriate punctuation marks and lets you see clever ways of formatting sentences.

- It helps you learn to write and speak grammatically correct English;
- It helps you build vocabulary;
- It gives you things to write about should you want to write a book;
- It helps you think critically—and more!

Television

I will share something else with you. I do not watch television, and I am not saying that you shouldn't. Well, to be truthfully honest, I *rarely* watch television. I just don't. Many people ask me why I don't watch TV. The answer is, I am just not interested in watching TV. Another reason is I have attention and impulsive issues (kind of similar to ADHD). So I can't sit still on a couch staring at a television screen for more than 20 minutes at a time (unless it is something that I am extremely interested in). This is the attention issue—I just can't pay attention and concentrate on the theme of a movie for longer than 20 minutes or so. I could watch a movie, but after so long of watching it, my brain will start thinking about other things that are more interesting to me. By the time I refocus to watch the movie, I am usually lost and have no clue what is going on. I usually ask my wife what is going on and why certain things are happening. This is because of my attention span.

I say that I am impulsive because when I get an idea about something, I feel the need to act on the idea, immediately. I usually write the idea down or think about the idea for prolonged periods. Because of this, I usually miss important components of the movie I am watching. Also, when I watch movies, I often get clever ideas about education and groups, and I begin thinking how to tie certain things from the movie into my groups. As a result, I have a difficult time following movies that last for hours.

In my spare time, I hang out with my wife and kids, and when I am not doing that, I am either reading books or writing. I read and write every day—which is how I became masterful at writing books within a short period of time.

My Challenge to You

Here is my challenge to you. If you want to be successful in life, you have to do something about it. No one will make you successful; no one will give you the world. You have to start right now on developing yourself and building your skills. You have to begin reading more, writing more, and applying yourself in the classroom. Applying yourself means engaging in the classroom. Remember, I defined engagement in Chapter 4. Engagement means applying yourself in the classroom. It means you will think about questions (cognitive engagement), raise your hand to ask questions, answer questions, and take notes (behavioral engagement), and find some way to enjoy learning (affective engagement).

In the "About the Author" section of this book, you will learn that I am a success coach. To understand what a success coach does, take a quick moment to think about a basketball coach and basketball players. Basketball coaches—all coaches for that matter—train and help their players build skills and become more knowledgeable about their game. That is what a success coach does. They work with clients (players) to help them build skills to achieve goals and to become successful in various areas of their life.

Professionals pay me big bucks to help them become successful.

Now, here is the good news. I will act as your success coach within this book. You could refer to me as Coach Williams. When I work with professionals on helping them become successful, before I start working with them, I explain the purpose of success coaching and eventually have them to sign a contract stating that they agree to read books that I recommend and apply the skills that are discussed during our sessions.

I have them to sign contracts because, as I explained earlier, there is a formula to success. Part of the formula is involving yourself, reading, writing, and applying skills on a daily basis. I will do the same for you. If you are willing to accept me as your success coach, I want you to sign and date your name on the space that I provide for you.

But before you sign, I want to share with you the benefits of working together, the benefits of being your coach. Okay—are your ready?

Cool—

- You will commit to reading this entire book.
- You will commit to applying the skills that I discuss in this book.
- You will email me throughout the weeks to let me know how this book is helping you become successful as a student (this could be a simple 1- to 2-sentence email at my email address: dwayne@ tier1education.com).
- You will explain to your teachers and parents/guardians that you are working with a success coach.

That is it! If you agree to this, then we will form a coach-player relationship. Now, I will coach you throughout this book. This coaching process will be simple. All you will have to do is read this book (I will speak to you throughout this book and give you recommendations), write your ideas down in this book, and email me throughout the week about your experiences.

If you agree to allow me to coach you through the process of becoming successful, I want you to sign and date here:

_____   _____

Sign   Date

I am hoping that you signed and provided the date, because from working with me, you will learn a ton of things that will help you become successful. You will learn things that, if you do what I recommend in this book, there is no doubt about whether or not you will become successful! If you signed and dated the above agreement, I want you to take a screen shot of your signature and date, save it to your phone, and email it to me.

If you have decided not to sign the document to allow me to work as your coach, feel free to give this book back to the person who gave it to you. I do not want to waste your time.

If you signed your name, let's get started!

Summary

When students earn high GPAs and solid grades, it is not because they were born super smart. Rather, in most cases, it is because they practice; that is, they study and complete their homework. In the same likeness, when students obtain extremely low GPAs and fail tests and quizzes, their failing is not because they are not smart, or born as unintelligent babies. Rather, they fail because they do not apply themselves; they do not study or practice.

In this book I shared with you my story in which I failed continuously as a student. The main reason I failed is because I rarely ever studied. I did not invest time in practicing the skills I was required to learn. If you often fail your classes or do not obtain the kind of grades that you desire, one reason for this is that you may not be investing enough practice hours to get the grades that you desire; you should never think that you are unintelligent because of poor grades, low test scores, and a low GPA. Usually, such performance happens when you do not invest enough time practicing the skills you are required to learn.

What's Next?

In the next chapter, I will begin with the importance of goal setting. I will introduce a goal setting chart and explain why setting goals is key to achieving success!

CHAPTER 6: CHARTING YOUR SUCCESS

Now I could let these dream killers kill my self-esteem
Or use my arrogance as the steam to power my dreams
*I use it as my **gas**, so they say that I'm **gassed***
But without it I'd be last, so I ought to laugh
—Kanye West, "Last Call"

In his song, "Last Call," Kanye West provides a vivid illustration of what his life was like prior to signing a deal with Roc-A-Fella Records. Prior to signing his deal, Kanye explained that he hustled his demo to different record labels only to get shot down with an abundance of rejections. In this song, he explains that he had a plan, a goal to get signed. He wanted a record deal, and he wasn't going to stop hustling—shopping his demo around to different labels—until he signed one. He called those individuals who didn't believe in his music "dream killers" and explained that he used his arrogance as his "gas" to keep him moving.

In this chapter, I talk about gas, but not the kind of gas that kept Kanye pushing his demo tape. The gas that I will discuss in this chapter stands for the **g**oal **a**ttainment **s**cale (GAS), which is an effective tool to use when creating goals. The tool allows you to document and determine if you met your goal.

Many of my former students explained that they didn't like Kanye because, although he is amazingly talented, they thought he was overly cocky and arrogant. My response has been, no matter how cocky and arrogant you think he is, the fact is, he is a genius. I often use Kanye

West's story to discuss the importance of determination and goal setting. Kanye was determined to get signed, as he described in his song, *Last Call*. Even more, he was a goal setter. He mastered his craft because he not only set goals, but also, he worked to either meet or exceed his goals. He did not settle for less.

When was the last time you set a goal?

If you set a goal recently, did you strive to meet or exceed the goal?

Goal Attainment Scale

In this chapter, I will discuss the importance of creating and measuring goals. For this book, I will refer to the *goal attainment scale* and use Kanye West's experiences with moving his demo as an example of creating goals. I will use "GAS" for short when referring to the goal attainment scale.

I'll share a funny story with you about the GAS tool.

When I introduced the GAS to my colleagues to use with their students, my colleagues made many jokes about having "gas."

The very next day after introducing the GAS tool to my colleagues, I arrived to my office about 45 minutes prior to the time I was supposed to be there. I had gotten up early that morning and wanted to get some things done before the school day started, so I went in early. When I arrived to my office, I noticed a piece of newspaper taped to the glass window of my office.

As I got close enough to read it, I laughed out loud! The newspaper was a "GASx Extra Strength" advertisement document. If you have never heard of this, GASx is used for people who experience discomfort—or a bloating feeling in their stomach—in response to gas. GASx apparently helps with this bloating, gas condition.

They had jokes!

Whenever we created goals for and with our students, my colleagues would say, "Hey, Williams, do you have gas?" then would laugh loudly. They would ask if I had gas instead of asking if I wanted to use the GAS tool to document goals for our students.

Warning

I will introduce the GAS in this chapter. So be sure that you do not eat too many beans, broccoli, cauliflower, or cabbage as you are finishing up this chapter; these foods increase the likelihood that you may need to pass gas, and possibly require GASx to control your condition!

Kanye West

As I explained earlier, I like to use Kanye West as a reference when discussing the need for goals. I like to use him as an example because the brotha' is extremely motivated and goal oriented when it comes to achieving success. Among all of his cds, *College Dropout* is my favorite, hands down. I love this cd for many reasons.

One of the best things I like about *College Dropout* is that Kanye discusses, in many songs, his struggle with achieving success. He talks about working countless hours on improving his craft; he talks about working at the GAP clothing store prior to signing his record deal, and his day-to-day struggle at the Gap; he talks about sitting and waiting for his spaceship to arrive; he talks about teachers telling him that he needed to be placed in "slow" classes. For example, after talking about all of the success that he had received after putting in hard work, he reflected on what he had achieved and said this:

> *"Now tell my momma I belong in that slow class . . ."*
> —Kanye West, "We Don't Care"

In *College Dropout*, Kanye makes it clear that he is not an overnight celebrity. He shows that he worked hard to get where he is in life. In the VH1 episode, Kanye's mother, Donda West, explained that Kanye became so passionate about making music and setting goals that he would lock himself in a room for days where he made beats. The documentary showed that Kanye was invited to meet with executives from Columbia Records, and although he thought he would finally sign a deal and break through the music industry, Columbia slammed the door on him; they refused to sign him.

How do you think this made Kanye feel? What do you think he did directly after leaving New York and Columbia records?

In response, Kanye returned to Chicago. Interestingly, Kanye did not give up when Columbia refused to sign him. In fact, the documentary showed that Kanye returned to Chicago with more motivation. It was reported that Kanye locked himself in the room for days, making beats. It was also stated that he did not party like he used to, go to clubs like he used to, or mingle with others like he used to. Rather, he remained locked in his room, in front of the keyboard, making beats.

Whoa! If that is not motivation to become successful, I don't know what is!

Getting rejected by Columbia Records led Kanye back to the drawing board. He made more beats, and began to start charging more money for his beats. He took his goals more seriously. His hard work and goal setting paid off. Through hard work, goal setting, and dedication, he eventually signed with Roc-A-Fella Records!

I'm the newest member of the Roc-A-Fella team . . .
—Kanye West

Kanye's work ethic speaks specifically to goal setting. His early life, prior to getting signed, is enough to inspire any young entrepreneur or person who desires to start a business or meet goals. His life shows that success does not happen to you; rather, you create it! His story shows that the ingredients to success include setting goals, working hard, failing, bouncing back, returning to the drawing board, revising goals, measuring whether you have met your goals, and beginning the process again.

Goal Attainment Scaling

Let's talk about the GAS tool that we will use to begin creating our goals. The GAS is a very easy tool to use with just about whatever you want to create goals for, and you could make yourself look impressive by teaching your teacher how to use it!

You could use the GAS chart to create goals for

- sports—to increase your shots per basketball game, to rush for more yards in a football game, to increase your speed in the 100 yard dash, and so on;
- academics—to improve your grades, to turn in homework assignments, and to do better on tests and quizzes;
- school attendance—to get to school on time, to get to class on time;
- referrals—to reduce the amount of referrals that you currently receive—and more!

This Is How the GAS Chart Looks

Don't panic! I will explain how to use this chart. And trust me, it is not complicated. Also, your teacher may have a teacher version of this same book. The teacher version has a GAS scale in it, and if your teacher has it, then you two could work together to figure out how to use it.

The GAS Tool

Rating	Current Level	Possible Outcomes	Goal	Goal Attainment
+2		Much more than expected		
+1		More than expected		
0	?			
-1		Less than expected		
-2		Much less than expected		

The chart on the previous page is how the GAS looks. It will be *extremely* easy to use once you figure it out, and the good news is you could use it with any goal you create!

We Will Follow 4 Basic Steps to Use the GAS

> **Step 1.** Pick a behavior (or something) to either *increase* or *decrease* (current level column).

> **Step 2.** Identify the possible outcomes you could achieve (possible outcomes column).

> **Step 3.** Pick a goal (goal column).

> **Step 4.** Weeks later, see if you met your goal (goal attainment column).

Let's Use an Example to Figure This Thing Out!

Let's use a basketball example to make it super easy. Imagine that you play basketball for your school's team. You have been averaging 16 points per game. You want to increase your points per game because you want more college scouts to look at you and you want to get more attention from the media.

So you want to create a goal and find some way to measure if you have met your goal. You begin to ask around to find a good system to use to help you create and measure goals. After chatting with your teacher and coach, and finding out that they do not have any systems to recommend, you remember reading this book, and remember the GAS chart! You remember the four steps. So you begin to plug away with filling in the chart.

Step 1—Current Level Column: Pick a behavior, or something to change. For this example, the behavior or thing that you want to change is your *average score*. So the first thing you want to do is put a 16 to the right of the zero in the Current Level column. You will not write anything else in this row, just the 16.

Do you know why you wrote a 16?

Well, because that is your current level of performance; it is your score before you create your goal. Usually when you create goals, it is a good idea to create the goal based on your current level of performance. So since you are currently scoring 16 points per game, you could create goals based on this score.

Step Two—Possible Outcomes Column. Identify possible outcomes you could achieve. To do this, simply look in the next column (you've already completed the Current Level column, now go to the next column)—the Possible Outcomes column. You will see that in this column you could either increase your score or decrease your score. Notice that you will have to look at your current score to see how much progress you will choose. So let's look at this.

Your current score is 16 (current level).

Now you can choose four Possible Outcomes (+1, +2, -1, -2):

> Possible outcomes:
>
> +2 = 20
>
> +1= 18
>
> Current score is 16:
>
> -1= 14
>
> -2 =12

Choosing the +1 option

> *You currently score **16** points a game.* You choose to score 2 additional points to go from 16 points to 18 points a game (16 + 2 = **18**). If you choose a goal of scoring 2 additional points (which is more than expected), then you would put an X in the goal column next to +1.

Choosing the +2 option

> *You currently score **16** points a game.* You could choose to score 4 additional points, in which case you would go from 16 points to 20 points (16 + 4 = **20**). If you choose to score 4 additional points, which would be "much more than expected," then you would put an X next to the +2, in the goal column.

Your score could decrease, too.

Choosing the -1 option

> *You currently score 16 points a game.* You could choose to score 2 points less than your average, in which you would go from 16 points to 14 points, (which is less than expected), then you would put an X next to the -1, in the goal column.

Choosing the -2 option

> *You currently score 16 points a game.* If you choose to score 4 points less than your average, in which you would go from 16 points to 12 (16 − 4 = **12**), which is much less than expected, then you would put an X next to the -2, in the goal column.

And yes, I know exactly what you are thinking. "Why would I choose to score fewer points?" Yep—I knew it and I'm not even a psychic! You may never choose to score less, but you know how it is, no matter how many shots you throw up, some hit the backboard and roll to the left or right, instead of down the middle and through the hoop.

Notice that if you pick the +1 row (+1 in Possible Outcome), you pick to increase your average by 2 points (16 plus 2 = 18). If you pick +2, you pick to increase your average by 4 points (16 +4 =20). Got it? Notice that you always start at your current level, which is 16. You would expect to average 16 points, since this has been your average score.

Step 3—Goal: Pick a Goal.

When you pick a goal, simply look at the Possible Outcomes column (to the left of the Goal column). Based on the possible outcomes, pick a goal. Let's say that you want to create a goal of scoring 20 points a game. Since this is your goal, then you would put an "X" in the goal column, right next to "20." Simple, eh? Cool!

Now, you could fill in steps 1-3 right when you sit down to fill in the chart. You could fill these in because you will already know the behavior or thing that you want to change (step 1); you could create *possible outcomes* based on how much you want to challenge yourself (step 2); and you could put an X in the goal column based on the goal you want to create.

What Will You Do to Meet Your Goal?

You probably know the saying, "If you continue to do what you have always done, you will get the same results that you have always gotten." Since this is true, if you do not make any changes to improve your score from 16 to 18 or 20, then perhaps you will never reach your goal. Since this is true, you will have to come up with a strategy. You could choose the following strategies to improve your score:

- Shoot 50 free-throws a day.
- Shoot 50 jump shots a day.
- Run 2-5 miles a day to increase your endurance and stamina.
- Get back in the weight room so that you could be a beast in the paint.
- Place cones or chairs on the court, and do dribbling drills around the cones and chairs, and shoot lay-ups once you reach the basket.
- Maybe you want to start eating healthier.
- Talk with your coach about allowing you to become more active offensively.

Whatever you choose as your strategy to increase your score, you want to use that strategy, or multiple strategies, for about a week or two. After you train yourself by using these strategies, you will document how many points you scored in your next game. Let's say that you have practiced the 50-free-throw and 50-jump-shot strategies. You enter your next game and you knock down 10 2-point jump shots. If this happens, then guess what, you met your goal—20 points!

Let's say that you hit 9 jump shots—well, then you hit 18 points and you didn't necessarily meet your goal. But check this out: Although you didn't meet your goal of 20 points, guess what? You still made progress! You went from scoring 16 points to 18 points!

Step 4—Goal Attainment: Put an X or your score next to: *Goal Attainment Column* based on the amount of points you scored. Let's say for example that you score 17 points. If this is the case, then put a "17" in the goal attainment column, (in the zero row).

Take a look at the chart below. If you forgot a step, then go back and re-read each step. It is important that you understand how the GAS chart works, because you could use it when you create goals in your hip-hop SEL group.

Rating	Current Level	Possible Outcomes	Goal	Goal Attainment
+2		20	X	20
+1		18		
0	16 points			
-1		14		
-2		12		

Review:

The Rating column allows you to create a goal that is *more* than expected (+1), *much more* than expected (+2), *less* than expected (-1), and *much less* than expected (-2). If you pick a goal that is less than expected or much less than expected, then you are not being ambitious at all. In fact, you are not challenging yourself. The goal should be to at least pick a goal increase of +1 (more than expected), or +2 (much more than expected)—then work your butt off to meet that goal. Once that goal is met, then you should start over and continue creating goals until you are scoring 50 points a game, based on the above example!

The Current Level column is where you put your current score, or performance. This could be your current points per game, a science grade, math grade, English grade, statistics grade, number of punches per boxing round, number of take downs in a wresting match, number of times you swear at your brother, number of times you skip class, number of times you turn in your homework, number of times your girl friend, boy friend, or best friend pisses you off—whatever!

During the time I was writing this book, the Cleveland Cavs and Golden State Warriors were competing in the NBA finals. At the time of this chapter, Lebron James was averaging 40 points per game! If he were to use the GAS chart to create goals to increase his points per game, what do you think he would put in the current performance column?

The Possible Outcomes column is where you would create possible outcomes for yourself. Remember, +1 would be a small increase from your current performance, and +2 would be a larger increase from your current performance (or whatever your think is reasonable and achievable). Negative 1 would be a small decrease from your current performance, and -2 would be a larger decrease from your performance. Notice how the possible outcomes correspond with the current score.

The Goal column is where you put an X in the goal space you plan to achieve.

Goal Attainment column is where you check or write your performance score in the space provided.

Remember, when you use this chart, you will always start in the Current Performance column, next to the number zero.

Can you use the GAS chart by yourself now? Let's try. I will give you an example and I want you to fill in the chart. Let's use Lebron James as an example.

King James

At the time that I wrote this chapter, Lebron was averaging 40 points per game during the 2015 NBA Finals against the Golden State Warriors. He wants to maintain or increase his average. If he maintains his average, then cool—he averages 40 points per game. If he increases his average, then even better! Your GAS chart is below. I want you to fill in the chart. Complete the chart based on your own make-believe example. Once you fill the chart in, use the space below the chart to explain your chart and explain each column.

Rating	Current Level	Possible Outcomes	Goal	Goal Attainment
+2				
+1				
0				
-1				
-2				

Use the space below to jot down the story you used for the example, and to provide feedback on the GAS chart and columns.

Now I will complete the chart based on Lebron James's goals and performance.

Rating	Current Level	Possible Outcomes	Goal	Goal Attainment
+2		42	X	
+1		41		
0	40 points			
-1		39		
-2		38		X

The first thing I did in this example was put "40 points" in the **Current Level** column. After that, I created **possible outcomes** (this could be whatever you want, based on your goals) that Lebron could achieve. I increased the score of 40 by 1 (+1 is 41, +2 is 42); and decreased the score of 40 by 1 (-1 is 39, -2 is 38). Notice that, at the very bottom of the Possible Outcomes column, you should be able to count without skipping around. In this example, you could count: 38, 39, 40 (40 was Lebron's average), 41, 42. In the example where you scored 16 points a game, you could count by 2s in order: 12, 14, 16 (16 was your current score), 18, 20.

Next, I put an "X" in the **Goal column**, next to 42 because I wanted to create a goal of Lebron averaging 42 points per game. Well, he didn't average 42 points per game. By the end of the finals, he averaged 38 points (I am not sure if he actually averaged 38 or not). He did not meet his goal, but he sure did perform phenomenally! Because he averaged 38 points per game, I put an X in the goal attainment column next to 38, which is much less than expected (-2).

You Should Be Good by Now!

With the many examples that I provided, you should be good by now. You should be able to use the GAS chart by yourself at this point. It is very important that you understand the idea of the GAS chart to create and measure goals because, as explained, you could use the chart in your SEL group, or when creating personal goals. In fact, this chapter is perhaps one of the most important components of this book. The reason is because creating and measuring goals is essential to developing skills

Summary

When I run my hip-hop groups, I often use Kanye West's story as an example of the importance of dedication, grit, and goal setting. In his cd, *College Dropout*, Kanye talks about how his life was prior to landing a record deal. Although he was rejected many times, he did not let his rejections dissuade him or give up on his dreams to produce and rap. Rather, rejection was the motivation that helped him try harder. One of the things that allowed Kanye to become successful at landing a record deal was his goal setting.

It was stated that when Columbia Records rejected Kanye, that he locked himself in his bedroom all day and made beats; his goal was to become better. In *College Dropout*, he says, "I deserve to do these numbers!" He explained that he deserves to do the numbers—to sell many records—because he put in the time, he dedicated himself, and he created and worked toward his goals. Be sure to use the GAS chart when creating and measuring goals. Remember, you could use the GAS chart when creating any goal. If you forget how to use it, be sure to return to this chapter to review the steps.

Good luck!

What's Next?

In the next chapter, I will explain the five skills that you will need to know to become successful and to meet every goal in your life.

CHAPTER 7: YOUR CHANCE AT FAMILY FEUD!

I don't rehearse on either of my shows, 'Family Feud' or my talk show. I never rehearse with the guests. I don't want to have any preconceived thoughts, notions, because that kills my creativity as a host and as a stand up.
—Steve Harvey

Lately, I have been watching the American game show, *Family Feud*, with my wife and children. I'll admit that we have been watching this show consistently for the past few months. I believe I have acquired an unusual addiction to watching it. The increase in our watching the show is a result of the game show host, Steve Harvey, who has a way of making simple comments amazingly funny!

Do you watch this show?

The idea of *Family Feud* is that families meet on the show and compete against other families; each family is a team who competes against the other team family. Family members are required to provide answers to questions that were posed to 100 people. The family who could accurately provide the same answers that the 100 people provided wins cash and the opportunity to win a car.

Similar to *Family Feud*, I have asked 50 students 5 questions, and have recorded their responses. I will ask you the same questions that I have asked the other 50 students and will give you the opportunity to guess the top 5 responses those students provided; the 50 students included freshman through senior males and females.

Are you ready? Cool—here we go!

Name 5 Things You Need to Achieve Success

Again, I have asked 50 students this question. I want you to write your responses on the lines below. What do you think were the top 5 responses among the 50 respondents? Be sure to provide your responses based on what *you think* were the top 50 responses among the freshman through senior students who answered them. So you will guess their responses, which may or may not be the top five thing *you* think you need to achieve success. All right, provide their responses below.

1._____

2._____

3._____

4._____

5._____

Cool, the top responses, among the fifty students, were

1. Work Ethic
2. Education
3. Intelligence
4. Money
5. Common Sense

Did You Accurately Guess Their Responses?

Did you guess any of the above responses? How do you feel about the top 5 responses that were provided among the 50 students?

The reality is we need many things to become successful, including intelligence, education, work ethic, and so on. I often ask this question when I meet with students to see what they think they need to become successful, and consistent with the 5 responses that the 50 students provided, many of my students say money and education, among other things. Some say "good grades."

Years Ago We Thought That Intelligence and Good Grades Were the Best Predictors of Success!

Years ago we believed that *intelligence* and good grades were the greatest predictors of future success. That is, psychologists thought that people who had high IQs, good grades, and high ACT scores would be the most successful people around.

Well, guess what? We were wrong!

Although grades, GPAs, ACT scores, and intelligence are important, there are other skills that are as equally important, if not more important, than intelligence, grades, and ACT scores. And if you learn these skills, you will be able to improve your grades, score better on tests, including your ACT, and increase your ability to reason, which is exactly what IQ scores are all about. So what are these important skills?

Social Emotional Learning

These skills are called, social emotional learning (SEL) skills. Just as we use GAS as a shorter way for saying goal attainment scale" (see Chapter 7 for a review of GAS), we will use SEL as a shorter way of saying *social emotional learning.*

Got it? Good!

Although I will discuss many other things that lead to success, I will focus primarily on the five SEL skills. We will set goals to become familiar and aware of these five SEL skills. This is our main goal—to become aware of SEL skills and we will use the GAS chart to create and measure our goals.

To become successful at anything in life, you will have to first become familiar with the "thing" you want to be successful at. You will have to know what that thing is, be able to define that thing and effectively explain what it is to others.

Again, the "things" that we will focus on are SEL skills and our main goal for this chapter is to become aware of what they are and what they mean. Before we discuss what these skills are, I want you to think for a moment about one thing that you will need to be able to accomplish the majority of your goals.

Although you need many things to become successful in life, if you could name only one thing that you will need to be successful, what would that one thing be? Write your answer on the space below. Remember, we definitely need more than one thing—in fact, we need an array of things to become successful—but I want you to think about this question and provide a response on the line below. If you could pick one thing only that you believe will lead to your being a successful student, and being successful at meeting your goals, what would that one thing be?

If I had to choose only one thing that I think would lead to my success in every area of my life, I would pick

_____.

Write your response above, the one thing you may need to be successful in life.

I will discuss this question below so be sure to write your response down before reading on!

At the start of this chapter, you had the opportunity to play a quick game of *Family Feud*, in which you guessed five things that students would need in order to be successful; you guessed based on how you thought the 50 students responded.

At this point, I want you to list five skills that *you* think will predict *your* success—five skills that will lead to success in *your* life. This prediction is similar to the *Family Feud* question. The main difference is, I want you to answer the question based on *your* own beliefs. Don't guess based on how you believe other students responded. I want you to predict what five skills *you* will need to be successful in every area of *your* life.

Predictions

Let's talk briefly about predictions to help you with this task. Predictions are things that you believe will happen in the future. If you toss a tennis ball against the wall, what do you suppose will happen? What do you predict? Do you predict that the tennis ball will stick to the wall? Do you predict that it will go through the wall? Or do you predict that it will bounce off the wall? I'd predict that the tennis ball would bounce off the wall, and I am sure that was your prediction!

Based on the above definition and the example, predictions are statements about what will happen or what might happen in the future. With this definition, I want you to name five things that you will need, five things that will predict a successful future for you. You could start your list by saying something like this: "In order for me to be successful now and in the future, I will need [fill in your five things]." You could also start by saying this: "To be successful now and in the future, I will need to be able to [fill in the five things]."

When you are predicting the things that will lead to your success, and thinking what to jot down on the lines below, don't think only about doing well in school, but also think about the key things you will need if your goal is to do well with sports, with rapping, with making beats, with earning As and Bs, with taking honors classes, with being more social and interactive, with managing your emotions, and with establishing relationships, among other things. Take a few minutes to think about this. Jot down five things that, if you were able to do them, you know you would be successful for the rest of your years as a student and would become a successful adult?

Ready? Go!

_____

_____

_____

_____

_____

Before moving forward in this chapter, be sure to jot down the five things that you will need that will predict a successful future for you!

Let's Review Your Responses

In the paragraph above, I asked you to choose one thing that may lead to success in your life. I would love for you to share that one thing with me via email. When you get a chance, please email me your response, as I can't wait to read your thoughts!

I am sure you may need whatever you jotted down. But here is what we know: If you have the ability to manage your emotions, you will be able to do great things in life.

You'd be unstoppable!

If you want to pursue a career as a successful rapper—yep, having the ability to manage your emotions may get you there! If you want to pursue a career as a basketball player—yep, having the ability to manage your emotions may get you there (and of course you'll have to have skills on the court, among other things—but managing your emotions is critical!). If you want to pursue a career as a lawyer, entrepreneur, psychologist, police officer, judge, social worker, teacher, whatever—having the ability to manage your emotions will predict whether you will meet your goal, among other things. In fact, there are many people who are amazingly gifted and talented. They have tremendous skills, but are unable to manage their emotions. When they become frustrated, they not only feel it, but also they show it! As a result, it is difficult for them the meet their goals.

When these individuals become emotional (upset or angry), they may

- swear at people,
- ignore people,
- skip work,
- skip school,
- give up on their dreams,
- refuse to complete an assignment in school or on the job,
- destroy relationships—and more.

If you don't remember anything from this book, remember this: The greatest predictor of whether you will become successful has everything to do with your ability to manage your emotions.

How well do you manage your emotions?

In addition to asking you to jot down the one thing that you think you will need that will lead to your success, I asked you to jot down five things that will predict your success. Again, please share your thoughts with me via email, as I can't wait to hear what you listed.

No matter what you included in your list, I am about to introduce you to five skills, skills that, if you master them, you will be most prepared to achieve every goal you attempt to achieve, if these goals are realistic and achievable; that is, you will be able to achieve any goal that is within your potential! These skills are social emotional learning (SEL) skills.

What Are Social Emotional Learning (SEL) Skills Anyway?

I will refer to a quote from the *Collaborative for Academic, Social, and Emotional Learning* (CASEL), the leading organization that addresses the social and emotional learning of all students.

> Social and emotional learning (SEL) is the process through which children and adults acquire and effectively apply the knowledge, attitudes, and skills necessary to understand and manage emotions, set and achieve positive goals, feel and show empathy for others, establish and maintain positive relationships, and make responsible decisions (CASEL, 2012, p. 6).

Based on the above definition, social emotional learning is a process of learning about yourself and learning how to function within your environments, while having the ability to manage your emotions, create and maintain responsible relationships, maintain awareness of your environment, and make responsible decisions as a teenager.

These skills are often broken down into five areas: (1) self-awareness, (2) self-management, (3) social awareness, (4) relationship skills, and (5) responsible decision-making.

Let's Take a Closer Look at These Skills

Again, I will refer to CASEL's (2012) definition, since many authors, teachers, social workers, and school psychologists refer to these definitions.

Self-Awareness: The ability to accurately recognize one's emotions and thoughts and their influence on behavior. This includes accurately assessing one's strengths and limitations and possessing a well-grounded sense of confidence and optimism (p. 9).

Self-Management: The ability to regulate one's emotions, thoughts, and behaviors effectively in different situations. This includes managing stress, controlling impulses, motivating oneself, and setting and working toward achieving personal and academic goals (p. 9).

Social Awareness: The ability to take the perspective of and empathize with others from diverse backgrounds and cultures, to understand social and ethical norms for behavior, and to recognize family, school, and community resources and supports (p. 9).

Relationship Skills: The ability to establish and maintain healthy and rewarding relationships with diverse individuals and groups. This includes communicating clearly, listening actively, cooperating, resisting inappropriate social pressure, negotiating conflict constructively, and seeking and offering help when needed (p. 9).

Responsible Decision-Making: The ability to make constructive and respectful choices about personal behavior and social interactions based on consideration of ethical standards, safety concerns, social norms, the realistic evaluation of consequences of various actions, and the well-being of self and others (p. 9).

Compare These Skills with the Five Skills You Explained You Will Need for Success

Prior to discussing the five SEL skills, I asked you to jot down five skills you believed would predict your success. Now I want you to compare the five skills that you wrote down to the five SEL skills that are defined above. Compare these skills below. First, take a look at the left side of the page and review the five SEL skills. On the lines next to each SEL skill, write down what you jotted down above. If you wrote down any-thing that is closely related to one of the five SEL skills, place that word on the line, across from the particular SEL skill.

Ready? Go!

5 SEL Skills	*5 Skills You Jotted Down Above*
1. Self–Awareness	_____
2. Self-Management	_____
3. Social Awareness	_____
4. Relationship Skills	_____
5. Responsible Decision Making	_____

Take a minute to review the five SEL skills that are listed to the left, just above this paragraph, and compare those skills with the five skills that you jotted down—the skills that you believe will predict your success in life. On the lines below, jot down how the SEL skills are similar to or different from what you believe will predict your success. For ex-ample, the five SEL skills are all about developing yourself, your skills, your emotions, making good choices, and learning how to make solid relationships.

Do the skills you mentioned focus on developing your emotions, or do they focus on good grades, money, test scores, or other things? On the space below, compare what you wrote and the five SEL skills. Dis-cuss if the things you believe you will need to be successful are similar to or different from the five SEL skills. Explain how they are similar to the SEL skills or different from them.

Ready? Go!

_____

_____

_____

_____

_____

When writing down how your responses are similar to or different from the five SEL skills, did you focus more on intelligence, common sense, money, grades, and/or solid ACT scores? I am curious because most students—and even adults—place a lot of emphasis on tests scores, grades, and intelligence, but as you now know, perhaps the greatest predictors of how successful you will ever become in life depends on how well you are able to manage your emotions, and how willing you are at developing the five SEL skills that I mentioned above.

Check out the scenarios below to get a better understanding of the importance of managing your emotions and developing the five SEL skills—and why, often, your intelligence level or grades are not the best predictors of future success.

Tyrone, the Whiz Kid

Meet Tyrone. Tyrone is a 17-year-old African American male, who is preparing to graduate from high school. Tyrone's peers often describe him as a whiz kid. They call him whiz kid because he achieved a perfect score on his ACT, had a GPA of 4.0, and was amazingly gifted and talented. Often, he would correct teachers when they made mistakes about historical facts during class. Although Tyrone was amazingly smart and gifted, he didn't do as well in college as he did in high school. For example, Tyrone found himself very lonely and depressed. In college, Tyrone was not the only whiz person on campus. In fact, people in his program were just as smart as he was and they even outscored him on quizzes and assignments. In addition, not only were his college peers brilliant, but also they were extroverted, able to relate to others, able to make friends, and would go out on the town during the weekends.

During high school, Tyrone was all about his books. He did not socialize during lunch, go to sport events, or participate in extracurricular activities. Because of this, he found it difficult to make friends in college and, while his peers had fun during the weekends and mingled with other college students, Tyrone sat in his room after his classes and during the weekends. This was Tyrone's life as a college student.

Tyrone became depressed because he had no friends, and the more sad he became, the more he found it difficult to study and maintain As in his classes. On one occasion, Tyrone was so emotionally distraught that he was unable to study as he did in high school, and as a result, he earned a D- on his test. This wasn't the only test he earned a D in, however. At the end of the quarter, Tyrone earned a D in this class. This was devastating for Tyrone, for he had never received a grade lower than an A while in high school. Because of his D, Tyrone became even more emotional; his emotions interfered with his decision-making in which he stopped going to that class. As a result, Tyrone failed the class!

Because of his failing the class, Tyrone stopped going to other classes. He had very few people on campus to share his thoughts with because he felt uncomfortable opening up with other peers and adults, as he did not do this in high school. Tyrone became so stressed out in college, because he felt that he had no one to support him, that he dropped out of college after his second semester. Although he was amazingly brilliant in high school, and earned solid grades, his emotions interfered with his ability to be successful in college. In addition, he was lousy at developing relationships, lacked self-awareness, had a difficult time managing his workload in college, and made poor decision after poor decision, which resulted in his dropping out of school.

Question: How did the five SEL skills pertain to Tyrone's lack of success in college?

Consider Maria, an 18-year-old Latina

Maria had a difficult time in elementary school because of language issues. She spoke English as a second language. Because she struggled with her language skills, Maria was embarrassed to speak out in class. During her middle and high school years, she agreed to participate in hip-hop social emotional learning groups where her teachers used music to teach the five SEL skills. From this group, Maria learned to manage her emotions, and learned how to respond positively when she felt that things weren't going the best way for her.

Because of this group, Maria became very self-aware in that she understood the things that made her upset, and she learned how to respond when she became emotional. She also became familiar with her strengths and weaknesses, and learned about the importance of establishing relationships with her teachers and other adults to develop her weaknesses. From this group, Maria became better at public speaking and learned strategies to help when she became anxious about things that were difficult to overcome. Maria graduated from college and enrolled in a university. Maria was a leader in her college classes. She asked and answered questions when others were afraid; she presented in her classes with confidence; she made friends and created solid bonds with her instructors.

Because of the relationships she had with her instructors, her instructors went the extra mile to ensure that Maria succeeded. They even helped her get a job, and wrote powerful recommendations for her to go to graduate school. When asked how she was so successful in college, Maria explained that she was not always motivated. She also explained that she was not the smartest person in the college program; she even said that she was not the smartest person in the room. She explained that, although she was not the smartest, she believed that she managed her emotions much better than most people her age, and that she was self-aware, socially aware, had the ability to manage herself, created relationships, and made good decisions.

She explained that she learned these skills in high school and now the skills had resulted in her doing well in college. She explained that, even if she doesn't perform well on a test or project, that she is able to manage herself and try harder next time. She explained that she learned in her hip-hop SEL program that failure is a part of life and is a huge part of success.

Based on the two different stories, what were the predictors to success in college? The answer is how well the students managed their emotions, and whether they developed the five SEL skills that I will teach you. The scenarios show that just because you have superior test scores, and good grades do not mean that you will do well in life. After all, you could have the highest grades, but an important question is, How well do you handle struggles and setbacks? You could get all As, but how would you respond if you failed a quiz or test? You could be the best basketball player in your conference, but how would you perform if your girlfriend cheated on you with your best friend?

Other questions:

- When you fail, do you doubt your abilities and worth?
- When you fail, do you give up?
- When things become very difficult, do you persevere?
- Do you have the ability to make relationships—and work with others?
- Do you have the ability to resist peer pressure?
- When someone says negative things to you about your race or culture, do you cuss them out and attempt to fight them?
- Are you aware of your environments and avoid parties and situations that could put your life and future career in jeopardy?

All of these questions pertain to the five SEL skills and if you could develop these skills, you will do amazing things in life, and perhaps achieve every goal you will ever create!

Here is a challenge that I have for you. I want you to memorize the five skills. The reason why I want you to memorize them is because I will refer to them perhaps in every chapter moving forward.

- **Self-Awareness:** being able to recognize your emotions, and how they influence your behaviors.
- **Self-Management:** being able to manage your emotions, thoughts, and behaviors in different situations.
- **Social Awareness:** being able to understand rules for behavior, and to recognize family, school, and community resources and supports.

- **Relationship Skills**: being able to establish healthy and positive relationships with others.
- **Responsible Decision Making**: being able to make good choices about personal behaviors and social interactions.

Try your hardest to memorize these five SEL skills. What approach will you use to memorize these? Perhaps you could memorize one a day. If you are ambitious, you may want to try to memorize all in one day.

At some point this week, I want you to share with others what you have learned about SEL skills. You could start this discussion by saying something like this: What do you think is the greatest predictor of success?

If the person you are asking doesn't understand what you mean, simply rephrase the question. Say this: What do you think you need in order to be successful in life? After they say things like good grades, intelligence, money, common sense, mentor, and other things that I am sure they will say, teach them about the importance of SEL skills! This is one way to memorize them; we memorize things better when we teach others about the things we learn.

Good luck with that!

Summary

Psychologists and teachers now know that having the ability to manage your emotions are perhaps the greatest predictors to success. The reason is, no matter how poorly you do in school, on the job, on your sport team, or wherever, you won't let negative emotions from your performance destroy you. Although you may become sad or overwhelmed about the situation, you will have strategies that will help you manage yourself, and will be more aware of making good choices and good decisions. In addition, you will understand the importance of establishing relationships with teachers and other adults to help you become the best person you can become.

What's Next?

In the next chapter, I will share why it is important for you to develop SEL skills. The reality is, you are getting older, you have feelings for others that you did not feel in elementary or middle school. You may have thoughts about sex, partners, and how your life will be once you graduate from high school and college. All of these thoughts are normal. In fact, it is a process of development. You are developing into a young man or young woman.

The problem is, although many students like you are developing into young adults, some students your age are unable to manage themselves and do not have strategies of how to overcome their fears, and are unable to manage their emotions. As you will see in the next chapter, many of these youngsters are committing suicide, dropping out of high school, having babies at an early age, and are struggling in life. You, my friend, can avoid these things by learning how to manage your emotions, choosing to make good decisions, making solid relationships with teachers and mentors, and developing socially and emotionally!

CHAPTER 8: WHY YOU MUST DEVELOP SEL SKILLS

If your emotional abilities aren't in hand, if you don't have self-awareness, if you are not able to manage your distressing emotions, if you can't have empathy and have effective relationships, then no matter how smart you are, you are not going to get very far.
—Daniel Goleman

For the next few minutes, I want you to think about your life. What do you usually think about throughout the course of a day? What do you and your peers usually talk about at lunch, in gym, over the phone, and when you all get up on the weekends? What are the stressors in your life? Stressors are things that may stress you out, like taking difficult classes, pressures of having to manage homework, keeping grades up, having to meet deadlines, making your high school's sport team, landing a starting spot on the squad, being accepted among other peers, and eventually preparing for life after high school.

Whew!

In addition to these stressors, you all deal with demands from your parents and teachers, in which they have expectations of you and hold you accountable when you do not meet these expectations. Come senior year, parents often drill students about what college they will attend, what kind of job they will consider, and what their plans will be now that they are approaching graduation.

As a school psychologist who has worked with youth for over 10 years, I understand how life can be stressful for you all. I have had students enter my office, sit in the chair across from my desk, look me in the eyes, and break down in tears. Both males and females have come to me with their problems, and their issues have led them to breaking down because they had no clue how to overcome their issues, manage their stress levels, or make it to the end of the week.

Some students break down because their boyfriend or girlfriend—the love of their life—cheated with their best friend. Others came to me because their parents divorced and they had to deal with the stress of their parents' divorce; other students faced threats of being kicked out the house if they did not bring their grades up; and some students were actually kicked out of their parents' house because of sexual behaviors, drug habits, poor performance in school, and other reasons. Students have come to me for support because their parent(s) or other relatives passed away and the students did not know how to deal with the loss.

Students have a lot to deal with and I acknowledge this. I get it, and this is one reason why I decided to write this book. When you go from elementary school to middle and high school, you all enter puberty and experience many changes in your bodies. You go from playing with trucks and Legos and wanting to attach to your parents all day, to spending more time with your peers, driving cars, and experimenting with life.

Life becomes even more demanding as you all attempt to find yourself, come to grips with your identity, and fit in with social-peer groups. There are many things that go on within the minds of teenagers:

- You all need to be accepted.
- You all want to be looked upon as cool.
- Many of the guys will do whatever it takes to avoid being considered a lame.
- Many females have to deal with how the media defines beauty, based on weight, body figures, and other things.
- You all experience a tremendous amount of peer pressure.
- Risky behaviors increase—including sexual behaviors, and experimenting with drugs and alcohol—and more.

How Well Do You Manage These Stressors?

Youth who are able to manage their stressors do so because they have some level of emotional intelligence; they are able to make good decisions, even when they are tempted to make poor choices. Others find it difficult to manage their stressors because they struggle with making good decisions when they are tempted. Think about yourself for just a minute. How do you deal with stress? Within a given day, you may be tempted by peers to do the following:

- show up late for class,
- skip class entirely,
- experiment with drugs,
- engage in sex, even unprotected sex,
- engage in risky sexual group activities,
- consider joining gangs or selling drugs,
- fight peers,
- bully and harass individuals who are less popular than you and your peers,
- steal from others,
- rob others,
- rebel against your parents' rules—and other things.

All of the above examples lead to negative consequences, consequences that could eventually jeopardize your life forever. How do you manage your behaviors? Did you know that approximately half of the deaths in the United States are caused by unhealthy behaviors that stem from our inability to manage ourselves, including our emotions? In fact, the first 10 years of the new millennium became known as the *decade of behaviors* (Martin & Pear, 2007). Can you guess why? Well, because people made extremely poor decisions and engaged in risky, unhealthy behaviors that caused many deaths. Making good choices could have prevented these deaths.

On the space below, I want you to jot down the names of people you know who lost their lives because of poor decisions. Think about the poor decisions of children, youth, and adults, whose behaviors led to their deaths, or to someone else dying. If you do not have any personal examples, think about what has been on the news; think about all of the shootings of Black males by police officers.

Think about the case of Trayvann Martin, Mike Brown, and Sandra Bland, among others; Google their names to refresh your memory about these cases. Write down the poor behaviors of others that led to deaths. Be brief. Don't write a lot. Just jot down the names of the individuals you know who died because of poor decisions that could have been avoided. Write their names, then the behavior that resulted in their death.

Ready? Go!

_____

_____

_____

_____

_____

Notice that all of the behaviors that resulted in the deaths of the people you named could have been avoided by making better choices and decisions. In the process of experimenting with life, many teenagers make decisions that ruin their chances at success, and some make decisions that lead to their death.

Let's take a closer look at the risky behaviors that many teenagers demonstrate; let's shed a bright light on why youth your age must invest in learning how to mange their emotions, make good choices, and develop social emotional learning skills.

Consider the following statistics on risky behaviors and their consequences. After reading the statistic, I want you to jot down on the lines below what SEL skill is needed to avoid that particular behavior.

I obtained the statistics from the Centers for Disease Control and Prevention (2010). You could go to the Centers for Disease Control and Prevention website and look these stats up and also look up other stats about teenagers.

Did You Know—

Suicide
For youth between the ages of 10 and 24, suicide is the *third* leading cause of death. It results in approximately 4600 lives lost each year.

A nationwide survey of youth from grades 9-12 in the U.S. showed that 16% of students reported seriously considering suicide, 13% reported creating a plan, and 8% reported trying to take their own life in the 12 months preceding the survey.

Each year, approximately 157,000 youth between the ages of 10 and 24 receive medical care for self-inflicted injuries at emergency departments across the U.S.

SEL Skills and Suicide Prevention and Interventions
Can you recall the SEL skills that are the focus of this book? How many can you recall? There are five of them. They include (1) self-awareness, (2) self-management, (3) social awareness, (4) relationship skills, and (5) responsible decision-making.

Now, think about the statistics above that are related to suicide. On the lines below, jot down which of the five SEL skills are needed to help prevent suicide and why that particular SEL skill is needed.

Ready? Go!

_____

_____

_____

_____

_____

HIV and Youth

Over 50% of youth in the U.S. who have HIV do not know they are infected?

In 2010, youth made up 17% of the US population, but accounted for an estimated 26% (12,200) of all new HIV infections (47,500) in the United States.

Youth, aged 13 to 24, accounted for an estimated 26% of all new HIV infections in the United States in 2010.

In 2010, Black youth accounted for an estimated 57% (7,000) of all new HIV infections among youth in the United States, followed by Hispanic/Latino (20%, 2,390) and White (20%, 2,380) youth.

An estimated 9,961 youth were diagnosed with HIV infection in the United States in 2013, representing 21% of an estimated 47,352 people diagnosed during that year. Eighty-one percent (8,053) of these diagnoses occurred in those aged 20 to 24, the highest number of HIV diagnoses of any age group.

At the end of 2012, there were an estimated 62,400 youth living with HIV in the United States. Of these, 32,000 were living with un-diagnosed HIV infection.

In 2013, an estimated 2,704 youth were diagnosed with AIDS, representing 10% of the 26,688 people diagnosed with AIDS that year.

In 2012, an estimated 156 youth with AIDS died, representing 1% of the 13,712 people with AIDS who died that year.

Now, think about the statistics above related to HIV and teenagers. On the lines below, jot down which of the five SEL skills are needed to help prevent HIV and why that particular SEL skill is needed.

Ready? Go!

_____

_____

_____

_____

_____

Car Accidents and Teen Deaths

One of the most exciting milestones of teenage years is obtaining a driver's license and being able to drive around the community, including being able to drive to school. I recall when I first obtained my driver's license and when I first began to drive. It was the greatest feeling at that time. But did you know that car accidents are the leading cause of deaths in teens within the U.S. (Center for Disease, 2010).

For example, reports state that

Seven teens ages 16 to 19 die every day from motor vehicle injuries. Per mile driven, teen drivers 16 to 19 are nearly three times more likely than drivers aged 20 and older to be in a fatal crash.

Remember, as you are reading these statistics, I want you to keep at the forefront of your mind the SEL skills that are the focus of this book. The goal by now is to have memorized them so that you could complete activities such as the ones above and the ones on the chapters that follow. As you did with the statistics above, jot down on the lines below the SEL skill or skills you think teenagers need to develop to reduce the number of car accidents a day, and eventually a year.

Ready? Go!

_____

_____

_____

_____

_____

Violent Behaviors and Teenagers

The Youth Violence Prevention at CDC reports the following (Youth Violence and Prevention, 2015):

Homicide is the second leading cause of death for young people between the ages of 15 and 24.

In 2010, more than 738,000 young people ages 10 to 24 were treated in emergency departments for assault-related injuries; over 30% of high school students reported being in at least one physical fight; and nearly 20% reported being bullied on school property.

Homicides and assault-related injuries among youth ages 10 to 24 in just one year cost Americans an estimated $16.2 billion in lifetime combined medical and work loss costs.

There are many cases where students have been bullied, and as a result, have committed suicide, have skipped school, or have experienced many issues with their health because of bullying behaviors.

Derrion Albert

Think about the unfortunate story of Derrion Albert, a 16-year-old male who lived in Chicago. Derrion was killed by a group of high school peers during a brawl that is believed to have been gang related. News reports at the time explained that Derrion was an innocent bystander. Youth who were involved in the murder of Derrion struck him with wooden boards. Four students were charged with his killing.

Michael Eugene

You may have heard of Derrion Albert's story when it happened, but are you familiar with the story of Michael Eugene, a 15-year-old African American male who was killed in 1989 over a pair of Air Jordan tennis shoes? Ironically, when he purchased his Jordans for $115.00, his grandmother didn't want him to wear the shoes to school. She knew that Michael's peers would harass him because of the shoes; she felt that they would try to take them. In response to her comments about wearing the shoes, Michael told his grandmother that his peers would have to kill him before he let them take his Mikes. His grandmother found it odd that Michael did not return home from school.

He was found dead, hanged barefoot in the woods.

What SEL skill do you think Michael's granny was aware of? Write your response here:_____.

As indicated by the Center for Control and Disease statistics, homicide is the second leading cause of youth between the ages of 15 and 24. On the lines below, jot down the SEL skills that you believe are needed to avoid being a victim of homicide and to avoid demonstrating aggressive behaviors when you become upset.

Ready? Go!

_____

_____

_____

_____

_____

High Risk Behaviors

Many of the deaths that occurred in the examples and statistics above resulted from high-risk behaviors. What are high-risk behaviors? These are behaviors that place the individuals demonstrating the behaviors in jeopardy of harming their future success, or at risk of losing their life. Do you believe good grades will help you avoid high-risk behaviors? What about high test scores in the areas of reading, writing, and math? How about a high GPA? Will a 4.0 help you to avoid high-risk behaviors? The answer is no.

High-risk behaviors are usually caused by making poor decisions and making poor choices when we are excited or frustrated. High-risk behaviors deal with emotions. Good grades, high GPAs, and high test scores are great and needed, but being able to ace a chemistry or geometry test will not help you manage your emotions when someone calls you a nigger, if you are African American, or if someone calls you a dehumanizing name in general.

In the hip-hop SEL groups that I ran, many African American males explained that if someone who is not Black calls them the N-word, that they would "whoop that person." In other words, they explained that they had zero tolerance for being called the N-word and that if someone who was not Black called them this, that they would fight them, and try their best to hurt them. When considering this scenario, what skill do you think the male students must develop?

_____

_____

_____

_____

_____

Now, think about the same scenario—the students who said that they would whoop anyone who called them the N-word. What SEL skills do you think they possessed or did not possess? On the lines below, explain the skills you believe the students possessed or did not possess, and provide reasons why you chose those skills.

Ready? Go!

_____

_____

_____

_____

_____

As indicated from this chapter, developing the five SEL skills are critical to success and are needed in order to meet the goals you create. Before moving into the next chapter, I will ask that you take a quick quiz. On the five lines below, name each of the five SEL skills. Don't look back at other chapters. I want you to pull from your mind the skills that you can recall, the skills that you can remember:

Ready? Go!

_____

_____

_____

_____

_____

If you were able to provide the names of the five skills, then that is awesome. If you missed a couple, then be sure to continue to rehearse them. It is important that you remember them. When you remember them, you could reflect on them throughout the day, and document how your choices and decisions were related to each skill.

The main purpose of this chapter was to make you aware of the importance of the five SEL skills and to show what could happen when students refuse to consider these skills. As with all skills, the five SEL skills do not develop on their own. Do you think Michael Jordan became perhaps the best player of all time by simply going to sleep, waking up—then, Kaboom!—enter MJ, one of the greatest players ever? No. Of course not! Jordan practiced.

The fact that he did not give up when he was cut from the basketball team in high school shows that he demonstrated *self-management* (he managed himself, his thoughts, and his emotions as he continued to practice to ensure himself a spot on the team the next year), *relationship skills* (he connected with others to learn how to improve his game), and *responsible decision making* (he did not shut down or throw in the towel when he got cut). Too many students give up when things become difficult or when things do not go their way. Think about the time you gave up when things didn't go your way. What happened? What did you do? What did you learn from that experience?

Summary

If your goal is to become successful in any area of your life—whether it is a successful student, a successful athlete, a successful author, a successful rapper, a successful producer—then you must develop the five SEL skills that are present throughout this book. You must be able to recognize your emotions (self-awareness), be able to manage yourself and your emotions in different situations (self-management), become familiar with what is going on within your community and how those things may affect you (social awareness), be able to create and maintain positive relationships (relationship skills), and be able to make good choices and decisions, even when you feel that you want to do the opposite (responsible decision making).

When you develop the five SEL skills, you will understand that you must complete your homework in order to obtain descent grades, remain eligible for sports, and eventually attend college (responsible decision making). We will all make poor decisions and choices at some point, but when we constantly make the same poor decision, then this shows that we must develop our willingness to make responsible decisions, which is one of the five SEL skills.

What's Next?

In the chapter that follows, we will begin discussing the idea of creating groups where you and your peers could meet to learn how to develop SEL skills together.

CHAPTER 9

Getting Started with SEL Groups
and Clubs in Your School

Start where you are. Use what you have. Do what you can.
—Arthur Ashe

Now that you are familiar with hip-hop SEL, this chapter focuses on how you could partner with your teacher, school social worker, or school psychologist to create these groups in your school. You could use the information from this chapter to help your teacher integrate hip-hop with instruction in the classroom. We learn best within groups and by practicing the things that we desire to learn. This means that, simply reading this book may not help you become better at managing your emotions or meeting your goals. Rather, this book will make you aware of SEL skills, and aware of the importance of managing your emotions.

If you are self-motivated and willing to develop SEL skills, this book will help you along the way. However, working in a small group with other peers and a teacher will help you become most successful with becoming better at managing your emotions and meeting the goals that you create.

Getting Involved in Your School's Activities

You probably know that some schools offer after school clubs for students. Some after school clubs include chess clubs, video gaming clubs, and other clubs to provide opportunities for students to get involved within their school's programs. You could talk with someone about starting an after school club that focuses on hip-hop and social emotional learning skills. To do this, you will need to have a teacher to sponsor the group. This just means that a teacher will be willing to stay after school and help you all run the group.

Before talking with someone about an after school club or program, you should meet with your principal about creating hip-hop social emotional learning groups that take place during the school hours. It is important that you explain that these groups will take place during the school hours because many students—and teachers—are unable to stick around after school.

Also, many teachers, school psychologists, and social workers offer groups within the school building during school hours to help students learn how to develop their emotions and social emotional learning skills.

So yes, that is where you want to start. Start with talking with your principal about your interest in creating hip-hop social emotional learning groups. In these groups, you and perhaps 7 to 8 other students will meet in a room and listen to hip-hop music while learning strategies of how to better manage your emotions.

It is important that you explain to your teachers that I have created a book specifically for them. The book shows them everything they need to know to run hip-hop SEL groups. In fact, the book provides lessons and scripts—word for word passages of what I have said when I ran my groups—that teachers, school psychologists, and social workers can use in their groups.

This means that teachers do not have to worry about creating anything; they do not have to worry about what they will say, what they will do, or how to get started. I do all of that for them in the teacher version of this book. I provide everything they need to know within the book. All they have to do is read the book and follow the steps that I have shared. Simple enough, huh?

Are you ready to get these groups started? Okay—here is what I want you to do.

Write a Letter to Your Principal

Write a short letter to your principal to share the idea of hip-hop SEL. It would be perfect if you could email your principal. If you cannot send an email, then simply write a letter and place it in her or his mailbox—or give it to the principal's secretary. In the letter, you should include your name, your grade level, and talk about why you are writing the letter. To make this process easy, feel free to copy the letter that is included below. In the letter below, you will have to insert your name in the space provided, after "my name is" and you will have to circle the grade that you are in: 9th, 10th, 11th, or 12th grade.

If days go by without hearing from your principal, be sure to follow up with him or her to explain that you shared the letter and that you are interested in feedback. Following up with your principal might mean going to his office and setting an appointment to talk.

Copy this letter to share with your principal. (Ask someone at your school if you could use the "copy machine" to make a copy of this letter.)

Hello!

My name is _____

_____

and I am a   9th, 10th, 11th, 12th grade student. I am writing you because I have been reading a book about how to manage emotions and how to develop social emotional learning skills. The book is called, "Like Music to My Ears: A

Hip-Hop Approach to Social Emotional Learning." The author of the book is Dwayne D. Williams. Mr. Williams is a school psychologist and teaches school psychologists, social workers, and teachers how to create social emotional learning groups that integrate appropriate hip-hop music. Hip-hop SEL groups are culturally relevant (youth culture).

I am reading the student version of the book, which is a book and workbook; he also wrote and offers a teacher edition of "Like Music to My Ears" that includes agendas, transcribed lessons that social workers, psychologists, and teachers could use, and appropriate rap songs that are aligned with the following 5 social emotional learning skills: (1) self-awareness, (2) self-management, (3) social awareness, (4) relationship skills, and (5) responsible decision making.

I would love to help start a hip-hop SEL group or club in this school and I have some ideas of how to do it, based on the student edition of *Like Music to My Ears* that I am currently reading. In the student edition, Mr. Williams, the author, shows readers how he worked with one of his students to create entertaining groups. He and his students called these groups "hip-hop SEL groups"—and now he uses his books to coach teachers and students on how they can create these groups within their schools.

Mr. Williams has agreed to make himself available to meet with us for a conference call whenever we meet. He explained that, if I email him or if you email him, that he'd be willing to meet via conference call or SKYPE to discuss setting these groups up.

I would love to be a part of these groups, as I am a fan of hip-hop and would love to learn how to manage my emotions and develop social emotional learning skills using hip-hop music. Is it possible to meet with you to discuss the idea of creating these groups at this school?

If so, please send a pass to my class so that I can meet with you to discuss this opportunity. It would be nice to meet with you, the school psychologist, and school social worker. Will you please set this up? Again, when we meet, I am hoping to get Mr. Williams on the phone to talk with us about creating these groups. I am really excited about this opportunity!

Again, my name is _____

And I am in the _____ grade.

Thank you and I look forward to meeting with you.

There You Have It!

There you have it. That is one of the best ways to get started with creating these groups in your school. Talk with your principal and these groups and let him know about the two different versions of this book.

Now, let's talk about what you should say when you meet with them. Prior to meeting with them, be sure to read chapter XXX, where I talk about how I met with one of my students and introduced the group idea with him. Share this story with your principals and teachers, and explain that you are willing to work with teachers, school psychologists, and social workers to help get these groups started. You should know that I created two separate books—a student and teacher version—so that students and teachers could work together. Here is why I did that: Many teachers are unfamiliar with rap music and may find it difficult to pair rap music with SEL instruction. Because this is true, they may be hesitant to use hip-hop within these groups.

Now here is the deal. School psychologists and social workers are very familiar with social emotional learning skills, but will need you to help them identify appropriate rap songs to pair with these skills. Again, in their version of the book, I have shared with them many songs that you all could use within your groups, but you should also share with them appropriate music that you all could pair with SEL skills.

Remember, there are 5 of these skills.
- Self-awareness
- Self-management
- Social awareness
- Relationship skills
- Responsible decision making

Collaboration

You should collaborate with your school psychologist, social worker, or teacher to help create these groups and to use hip-hop music to make these groups fun. You could also have your teachers email me with questions on how to make their groups fun and effective. I'd be happy to talk with them and to help you all get these groups started in your building.

Remember, in the letter that you will print and give to your principal, I explained that I will make myself available for a conference call or available via SKYPE when you all meet to discuss the group. During this time, I can help you explain to your principal the purpose of the groups, how the groups have helped students like you meet goals, and how you all could get started. If you have questions about this process, please don't hesitate to contact me at Dwayne@tier1education.com. Refer to the Appendix section to get a copy of the letter that is in this book that you should share with your principal. In the appendix section, I have also included fun activities that you all could include within your group to make the group time fun and entertaining. Some examples include having cyphers, writing lyrics, recording your music, uploading your music on YouTube, and so on.

Summary

It is great that you have read a book on how to manage your emotions and develop your social emotional skills. But simply reading this book may not develop your skills, meet your goals, or help you become successful. This book will help you become aware of the skills that you need to become successful.

If you are self-motivated and are willing to read more about SEL skills and work on becoming self-aware, work on managing your emotions, work on becoming socially aware, work on developing and maintaining relationships, and work on making better choices, this book may help you along the way. However, working in a small group with other peers and a teacher will help you become most successful with becoming better at managing your emotions and meeting the goals that you create.

To get these groups started, you should print the letter that is copied within this chapter and put it in your principal's mailbox. The letter explains that you'd like to create hip-hop SEL groups at your school and that you have ideas of how to do it. I will make myself available via conference call or SKYPE to talk with you and your principal to get you all started. Email me if you have additional questions. My email address is Dwayne@tier1education.com.

What's Next?

In the next sections, I provide another copy of the letter that you should print and share with your principal. I also include activities that you all could include within your groups to make then fun and engaging!

Letter to Your Principal About Creating Hip-Hop Social Emotional Learning Groups

Hello!

My name is _____

_____ and I

am a 9th, 10th, 11th, 12th grade student. I am writing you because I have been reading a book about how to manage emotions and how to develop social emotional learning skills. The book is called, "Like Music to My Ears: A Hip-Hop Approach to Social Emotional Learning." The author of the book is Dwayne D. Williams. Mr. Williams is a school psychologist and teaches school psychologists, social workers, and teachers how to create social emotional learning groups that integrate appropriate hip-hop music.

I am reading the student version of the book, which is a book and workbook; he also wrote and offers a teacher edition of "Like Music to My Ears" that includes agendas, transcribed lessons that social workers, psychologists, and teachers could use, and appropriate rap songs that are aligned with the following 5 social emotional learning skills: (1) self-awareness, (2) self-management, (3) social awareness, (4) relationship skills, and (5) responsible decision making.

I would love to help start a hip-hop SEL group or club in this school and I have some ideas of how to do it, based on the student edition of *Like Music to My Ears* that I am currently reading. In the student edition, Mr. Williams, the author, shows readers how he worked with one of his students to create entertaining groups. He and his students called these groups "hip-hop SEL groups"—and now he uses his books to coach teachers and students on how they can create these groups within their schools.

Mr. Williams has agreed to make himself available to meet with us for a conference call whenever we meet. He explained that, if I email him or if you email him, that he'd be willing to meet via conference call or SKYPE to discuss setting these groups up.

I would love to be a part of these groups, as I am a fan of hip-hop and would love to learn how to manage my emotions and develop social emotional learning skills using hip-hop music. Is it possible to meet with you to discuss the idea of creating these groups at this school?

If so, please send a pass to my class so that I can meet with you to discuss this opportunity. It would be nice to meet with you, the school psychologist, and school social worker. Will you please set this up? Again, when we meet, I am hoping to get Mr. Williams on the phone to talk with us about creating these groups. I am really excited about this opportunity!

Again, my name is _____

And I am in the _____ grade.

Thank you and I look forward to meeting with you!

Activities to Make Your Group Entertaining

Hip-Hip SEL Activities
- Cyphers
- "Give me words" freestyles
- Name that song
- Hip-hop debates
- "In the booth"—recording lyrics

- Produce videos and songs
- Upload lyrics, songs, and performances on YouTube
- Create tag names
- SEL, hip-hop, and STEM—show how hip-hop pertains to science, technology, engineering, and mathematics
- Guest performers (local artists)
- "Artist spotlight"—in which members identify an artist of the week, such as Drake or Kanye West—and discuss the artist's accomplishments and SEL skills
- "Hip-hop" projects
- Panels and discussions
- Visits to colleges
- School performance (pep rallies, variety/talent shows)
- Trivia games that pertain to hip-hop
- "Lyrical sessions"—writing sessions with instrumental music
- Weight training (after school club)
- Basketball (after school club)

If you have more activities, please email me your thoughts at Dwayne@tier1education.com. Also, I provide examples of the above activities at my website: www.tier1education.com

REFERENCES

Effective social and emotional learning programs: *Preschool and elementary school edition.* (2012). Collaborative for Academic, Social, and Emotional Learning, 6-9.

Fredricks, J. A., Blumenfeld, P. C., & Paris, A. H. (2004). *School engagement: Potential of the concept, state of evidence.* Review of Educational Research, 74(1), 59–109.

Centers for Disease Control and Prevention, National Center for Injury Prevention and Control. Webbased Injury Statistics Query and Reporting System(WISQARS) [online]. (2010, 2012, 2013). Available from http://www.cdc.gov/hiv/group/age/youth/index.html.

Centers for Disease Control and Prevention, National Center for Injury Prevention and Control. Webbased Injury Statistics Query and Reporting System(WISQARS) [online]. (2010, 2012, 2013). Available from http://www.cdc.gov/MotorVehicleSafety/Teen_Drivers/teendrivers_factsheet.html

Centers for Disease Control and Prevention, National Center for Injury Prevention and Control. Webbased Injury Statistics Query and Reporting System(WISQARS) [online]. (2010). [cited 2012]Available from http://www.cdc.gov/violenceprevention/pub/youth_suicide.html.

Youth violence prevention at cdc (2015). In *violence prevention*. Retrieved September 3, 2015, from http://www.cdc.gov/violenceprevention/pdf/youth-violence-accomplishments-a.pdf.

INDEX